The ABCDEFG DISORDER

A Heartless Diagnosis

Patricia Stroh

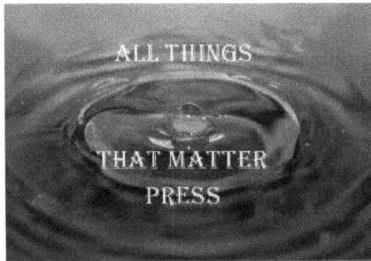

ALL THINGS

THAT MATTER
PRESS

The ABCDEFG DISORDER

ISBN 13: 9780990715849

Library of Congress Control Number: 2015931481

Cover design by All Things That Matter Press
Published in 2015 by All Things That Matter Press

This is a work based upon true events, however, some portions and names have been fictionalized.

This story is dedicated to all children who suffer with learning disabilities and the inability to develop the social cues necessary to live in our complex society, and to the parents who feel alone and ostracized by the community without direction.

Special thanks to my husband, Charlie, to the members of our family and dear friends who stood by us in the most difficult of times, to the counselors in the Ulster County Kids Together Program, the social workers at Onteora School District, the therapists, teachers and aids who worked diligently to help Derek succeed in the most difficult of circumstances, and to the powers that be for giving me my son.

PROLOGUE

It was hot and humid Sunday morning. Charlie went to the store for the newspaper and rolls while I prepared for our Sunday morning ritual. After the eggs and bacon were cooked, I called Derek to tell him breakfast was ready. He emerged from his bedroom, grabbed a plate of food, and ran back to finish playing a game on his X-Box. Charlie and I sat in the living room, read the paper, ate our food, and glanced at the Weather Channel.

"Charlie, what are you up to today?"

His answer was typical. "This and that."

"No shit. Really, what are you doing? Are you going on a bike ride?"

"Yeah, I'm gonna work around the house this morning and go on a ride this afternoon."

His ride usually took about two and a half hours so I knew I had to plan something with Derek that afternoon. He had spent most of the summer between eleventh and twelfth grades at home and without a license, a job, or close friends to hang out with, he was consistently bored.

After Charlie left for his ride I knocked on Derek's door, opened it slightly and stuck my head in.

"Do you want to go in the pool?"

"Not really."

"What do you want to do? Want to go for a walk?"

"No. Can we go to Al's and get something there?"

A trip to the farm stand wouldn't take long. The only plan I had was to be sure he made it to Bob's for training at 4:00.

I agreed. "All right, maybe I'll find a good cheese squash and we'll make a pie next week."

He shut the game down, bolted out of his room and followed me while I searched for my shoes. He sat on the bed next to me as I slipped my shoes on and walked one step behind me as we left the bedroom. He reached from behind me, put his arms around my waist, and clasped his hands at my stomach. I stopped and tried to pull away, but he had a pretty good hold. He gave me a quick squeeze and held tight. I tried to unclasp his hands but he was too strong.

"Come on Derek, cut it out. You're driving me crazy. Do you want to go to Al's or not?"

He let me go, laughed aloud, grabbed the car keys, ran out, jumped in the passenger seat, and turned the car on while I grabbed my purse.

While at the farm stand I found the perfect squash and Derek picked a few items. As we stood on line he tried to persuade me to buy more than I was willing.

"Mom, I'm really thirsty. Can I get two juices?"

"Derek, I am buying one. Put the other one back."

"Fine. So, I'll die of thirst."

"Derek, just put it back."

After I paid Al he admonished Derek for not offering to carry my bag to the car. He looked at Al with intensity, groaned a bit, and grabbed the bag.

Sundays always seemed to go fast and this one was no different. I had worked my way through the afternoon without paying attention to the time.

"Mom, it's time to go."

"Oh god, Derek, wait a minute. I have to write a check and a quick note to Bob." I rushed to find my checkbook and a piece of note paper, grabbed my keys and we were off.

When we got to his house I noticed other cars in the driveway. Bob was running a little late. So, as we stood waiting, I put my arms around him and said, "Derek, I'm so glad that you decided to go ahead with this training. I am so proud of you. You know, if you work really hard at this, your life will change for the better."

"Yeah, I know mom."

Within a few minutes Bob came out to greet us. He explained to Derek that they would be working on exercise and that they might have time to work with the swords. Derek's eyes lit up.

I turned toward him, looked up, and placed my hand on his chest and told him, "Do a good job kiddo, have fun and I'll see you around 5:00. I'm going over to Annette and Greg's for a while."

During my visit the three of us sat on the porch, sipping wine and expressing relief that our kids were doing well. Derek finally found his niche in school. He was determined to get in shape, earn his driver's license, and turn his life around. And, Annette and Greg were cautiously optimistic that their son would survive his first week of college.

I was so relaxed sitting with my friends on the porch that late September afternoon I didn't want to leave. After all, Bob was running late and he'd hang out with Derek until I got there. Little did I know my decision to linger would be one that I'd regret the rest of my life.

BEGINNINGS

I tossed between the sheets around 6:00 a.m. and peeked at the frost on the window. I could hear Jessica getting ready for school and wondered whether she'd grab the bus or walk. It was frigid outside with a forecast high of 14 degrees.

Charlie turned toward me and asked, "How are you feeling this morning?"

I was about a week past my due date and we were both anxious. It was precariously close to Christmas and we had hoped our baby would be born before that day.

"Okay, nothing yet, hon. Maybe today."

I was so tired of pregnancy. During the first three months I waited for signs of life. I'd look in the mirror to detect whether anyone would notice a baby bump. By the second trimester I had to unzip my pants on the way home from work and occasionally could be seen wearing a T-shirt that said "I'm Not Fat, I'm Pregnant." By the third trimester I felt and looked like I had a huge bowling ball emanating from my gut.

I was thirty-six years old with a thirteen year old daughter and a new husband. I knew tough times were ahead but dreamt of holding, nurturing and protecting this child. I was ready for the new chapter in my life.

By the time Jess yelled goodbye and ran out the door, Charlie was making an effort to get out of bed. He wanted nothing more than to stay in the confines of our warm home, but the crew planned to work on the house they were building in Woodstock.

After breakfast we made plans in the event I went into labor during the day. There were no phones at the job site so I'd have to call someone to drive there and get him. We agreed his mom would be our best bet.

Just before Charlie left for work I asked him to lift our Hobart mixer from the cabinet and put it on the counter for me.

I watched as he shook off the cold and got into the truck. Wasn't sure if he could see me through the frost on the door, but waved goodbye to him anyway. As he made his way out of the driveway and down the road, I considered my plans for the day.

I recalled my remarkable boost of energy the day before giving birth to Jessica. I raked the entire yard of leaves and twigs that were neglected for months, self-consciously forcing her into the world and causing the end of the third trimester.

This time around I'd be more patient: straighten up the house a bit, make a few batches of cookies, take a nap, and wait. As I turned to the kitchen I realized that Charlie forgot to put the mixer on the counter. It was a heavy commercial machine and I knew lifting it could jeopardize my health. But I really wanted to bake. I bent down, pulled the mixer ever so gently to the front of the cabinet and lifted it with the strength of my biceps.

After the last batch was made, I cleaned up and decided to lie down for a nap. Before falling asleep, I prayed, "Please little one, don't wait until Christmas."

Whether caused by the weight of the mixer, that self-conscious urge, or the natural order of pregnancy, my water broke during my dreams.

I called my mother-in-law, "Trudy, the doctor told me to get to the hospital. Would you get Charlie?"

"Sure, kiddo I'm on my way."

I called my mother and asked her to pick Jessica up from school and promised to call her after we spoke to the doctor.

A short while later, Charlie nervously walked in the door and asked, "Pat, are you sure we should be leaving for the hospital?" Are you sure your water broke?"

"I'm pretty sure. I can't imagine that it could be anything else."

"What did the doctor say?"

He said, "Get to the hospital."

We grabbed a few necessities, locked the door on our way out, and got in the car. The drive seemed endless and the memories of child birth thirteen years prior sent flashes of fear through my brain.

We arrived at the hospital about 1:00 p.m. and I was checked in. After being examined and prepped the nurse told us that it might be a while before I felt my first contraction. She suggested that Charlie might want to get a cup of coffee or a bite to eat before they started. He ran to a local drive-through and returned with a bag of fast food. I craved a bite of the cheesy grilled burger and greasy fries, watched as he ate every morsel, and contemplated the yummy drops of ice water allowed during labor.

We watched the news and the weather channel to deflect our nerves. Jeopardy had started when the nurse peeked in and said, "Mrs. Stroh, I just spoke to your doctor. If you don't start contracting by 8:00 p.m. he wants us to induce labor." Half way through Wheel of Fortune I felt my first contraction.

As they gained in strength and longevity, Charlie stayed by my side. He used all the techniques learned in class: placing ice on my head, massaging me through the pain, and comforting me in every way possible. I, on the other hand, forgot most of the lessons. My breathing became more difficult and my patience grew thin. I wanted my baby and I wanted it now. Screw the breathing, the melodic tones, the massages, and the ice.

As the sun began to peek through the shades, my doctor arrived. He glanced at the records, talked to us for a minute, and then examined me. "Pat, the baby seems to be in a precarious position. If I manually adjust it you should be able to deliver soon."

I agreed to the procedure and not long after I was instructed to push. I pushed as hard as I possibly could but nothing happened. Then he said, "Pat, I'm going to use forceps." As soon as the instrument was in place I gave a final push and, on December 23, 1989 at 7:04 a.m. our son was born.

I waited impatiently for them to clear his lungs and listened for the sound of his cry. It took longer than I thought it should and there seemed to be a hesitance when I asked if he was okay. One of the nurses replied, "Yes, he has all his fingers and toes. We are just going to give him a bit of oxygen."

"Is he going to be all right?"

"Yes," she said, "He will be fine," as she briskly carried him to the examination table. I heard the medical team speak as oxygen was administered but couldn't understand what they were saying. Within a minute or so I could tell that the oxygen had been removed and that they were testing his appearance, pulse, grimace, activity and respiration (APGAR). While my doctor examined me I could hear the results. They seemed concerned about his color. I tried to watch them but my vision was blocked. I held my breath and, after what appeared to be a few tense moments, I heard sighs of relief.

As they cleaned and wrapped our boy tightly in his blanket, one of the nurses asked if we had picked a name.

"Yes, we have. His name is Derek Robert."

She placed him gently on my chest and I felt the life Charlie and I created. Our son was a healthy 7.8 pounds. I turned him ever so slowly and marveled over his tiny face. I cupped my hand around the top of his head and kissed him softly. Charlie asked to hold him and I watched as he caressed our son. Time seemed to stand still.

When it was time for the nurses to move me to the maternity ward, I reminded them that I wanted to breastfeed as soon as possible. They promised to bring him to me as soon as I was settled.

Charlie followed behind as the nurses wheeled me to my room. They tucked me in after a quick exam and we waited for someone to bring Derek. It wasn't long before I heard a nurse wheel the bassinette into the room.

I watched intently as the she prepared to hand him to me. She checked his wristband and then mine to be sure we were a match and, just before she picked him up and moved toward my bed she said, "We had to give him formula. He was extremely hungry."

Trudy, my mother and Jessica were the first visitors to arrive at the hospital. Of course, they thought Derek was the most beautiful baby they had ever seen. The proud grandmothers were anxious to get their hands on him but rules were rules. Grandparents had to wait.

Jessica begged, "Please, can I hold him?" Charlie placed Derek in Jessica's lap and I watched my 13 year-old daughter envelope her brother. She looked at him intently as she touched his tiny fingers, creating the beginning stages of their bond.

Charlie and I had hoped to bring Derek home Christmas morning. I was anxious to be in my own home without the prodding of nurses and doctors and Charlie was tired of traveling in the bitter cold. After passing the jaundice test, the doctors believed Derek was healthy enough to go home.

While I dressed our little boy for his entrance into society, Charlie grabbed the infant seat, placed it in the car, and returned to the room for my clothes and gift bags. One of the nurses guided me into a wheelchair, handed Derek to me with a typewritten sheet of "Parental Instructions," then wheeled us to the exit where Charlie was waiting.

During the ride home we foolishly planned our Christmas day. Trudy was preparing turkey dinner for us and we were looking forward to a quiet holiday. As soon as we walked in the door Jessica begged to hold her brother, while Trudy had that "I want to hold my grandson" look on her face. They took turns cooing over him and, just as I held my arms outstretched to receive "my" baby I heard a knock at the door. My mom and her friend Chet couldn't wait to see him either and, of course, she wanted to hold her grandson, too.

They each took turns snuggling the baby as we exchanged Christmas presents. Then our gift to the world was carefully placed under the tree. Charlie took pictures of Derek as the family marveled over our most precious creation.

After dinner and a few more visitors we had the house to ourselves. Charlie, Jessica and I toasted Derek's birth with a glass of champagne. Then, much to my surprise, Charlie set off an amazing display of fireworks in honor of our son's arrival.

NO INSTRUCTIONS FOR THIS

Charlie stayed home with us for a few days before going back to work and Jessica was home from school for Christmas break. It was great to have them home, but I selfishly craved snuggling with Derek by myself. I was anxious to set up a routine without interruption, determined to breastfeed without complication.

Within a week it was more than evident that my breastfeeding ability stunk. I couldn't produce enough milk and I was afraid Derek would starve to death. I called the doctor's office and they arranged for a nurse to visit. When she arrived, I invited her to sit at the dining room table then retrieved Derek from his crib. After speaking with her briefly, she asked me to show her how he latched. It was odd for me to expose myself and the baby but she comforted me, gave me a few instructions, and promised me that we'd be fine. Days after her visit I knew neither of us were fine. Nothing seemed to satisfy him and I was tormented by my inability to calm him. He'd cry, then I'd cry, and Charlie paced. I wondered if he would ever stop.

One afternoon Charlie sat me down and said, "I know how upset you are and how much you want to do this but it's not making either of you happy. I'm getting formula." He did and, much to my dismay, Derek seemed to like the formula better than me. The crying stopped.

It had been thirteen years since giving birth to Jessica and I had conveniently forgotten feeling totally incompetent and exhausted. I forgot about recuperation time and the pain of actually giving birth. I forgot about the sleepless, worrisome nights, and the anxiety endured. So, the relentless, continual needs of my newborn made me feel as though I was going to lose it physically and emotionally. This "mommy" thing was not going to be easy.

I tried to stick to a routine. After feeding Derek I'd place him in his crib with the hope he'd gently fall asleep. I'd rub his back, then attempt to quietly remove myself from the room. Unfortunately, each time I reached the hallway he'd begin to cry. After a few attempts at calming him to sleep I'd give in. He slept well in my arms.

At times he'd cry so hard he turned purple. I had to give in. I'd hold and rock him for hours before he'd fall asleep. Not long after he was resting quietly he'd wake up hungry. My routine completely broken and my spirit drained, I called Derek's doctor and made an appointment to see him. I told him about my breastfeeding complications, Derek's inability to rest, his constant need for food and my parental abilities. The doctor explained that there was nothing wrong with the baby and that I should try to keep to a schedule. I left a bit more confident but the crying continued.

A few days after the doctor's appointment, Charlie called me into the nursery where he was changing Derek's diaper. "Pat, look at this. I think Derek has a hernia."

He showed me a lump on the side below his stomach, pressed it ever so slightly, and Derek began to cry. A few days later Charlie's diagnosis was confirmed and surgery was scheduled. During the post-operative appointment I was told that he couldn't have anything to drink after midnight and that we would have to use a pacifier to keep him content between that time and surgery. The thought of depriving him from food and sticking a pacifier in his mouth from midnight to 7:30 a.m. was horrifying.

The morning of surgery we dressed him quickly, placed him in the car, and did everything we could to keep him calm. By the time we arrived on the surgical floor he was less than satisfied with the pacifier and cried relentlessly while the nurses prepared him for surgery. As horrible as it was for our two month old to go under the knife, we were both relieved when he was taken to the operating room.

Everything went well. Charlie and I were led to his room where we watched over him. We were completely drained but prepared for him to wake. I held his bottle and waited for the first hint of movement and, as soon as he let out a sympathetic cry, I placed the nipple in his mouth. He was content and we were confident that Derek would feel better. He'd recover well from surgery, the crying would subside, and we'd be able to get some sleep.

I promised Charlie I'd go back to work when Derek turned three months old but I couldn't do it. I couldn't imagine leaving him in daycare. I convinced myself that the earnings I'd receive working in a law office would merely cover the cost of leaving him with someone other than me.

As I scanned the help wanted ads I wondered what alternative I had and began to put together a scheme to stay at home with my boy. One Sunday morning I saw a real estate ad boldly displayed in the classifieds and thought, I could get my license, sell some properties and stay close to home. In fact, I thought if I told my mother and grandparents about my idea they would be more than willing to watch Derek. Mom had moved in to Nana and Pop's after her divorce from her second husband. She needed a place to stay and they needed her help. Pop was showing signs of Alzheimer's and Nana was having difficulty walking after hip replacement surgery.

I knew my mom would be great with him and that Nana and Pop would feel as though they were Derek's caregivers. They'd spoil him completely. Mom would do the chasing while Nana and Pop smothered him with affection. It was the greatest plan I could conger and they jumped at the chance to watch him.

I spoke to the owner of the real estate agency around the corner from my grandparents' home and she agreed to give me a chance. She warned me that it could take a new salesperson about six months to put a sale together but I was determined to make it work

Within a month, I put together my first deal and things were starting to look up. If a client was interested in looking at property during the weekend I'd put Derek in his car seat, apologize to the clients, ask for their indulgence, and off we went. Derek in tow, I showed clients their prospective new home and, for the most part, did pretty well.

Before spring came to an end I had a couple of sales pending. As the temperature warmed and flowers bloomed, the tiny town of Phoenicia came alive. I was encouraged to see tourists walk by the office to look at properties for sale.

After a particularly crazy day of carting people all over the countryside, I was anxious to get home. As soon as I walked in the door I received a call from one of the couples I had been with earlier that day. I spent the next hour or so giving them the low-down on one of the properties I showed them while whipping up a quick dinner. By the time I hung up, Derek was fussing. Jessica helped me get our dinner on the table while I fed the starving boy.

In anticipation of a quiet, non-eventful evening I started to get Derek ready for bed. I brought him to the changing table, unsnapped his clothing, took off his diaper and began cleaning him.

As I went through the motions, I noticed a little lump just to the side of his belly. I grazed my hand over his skin and compared the lump with the little scar still visible from his operation. I called Charlie into the room.

"Look at this. Is it another hernia? Didn't the doctor say he wouldn't get one on this side?"

He examined the area, shook his head and sighed, "Damn it, I think it's another one."

We were completely dumfounded. The thought of having to experience this procedure again was devastating.

The next morning I called the doctor and within a week we were back in the hospital, going through the same anxiety and concern. Again, we had to withhold formula, stick the pacifier in his mouth, and pray. The poor thing screamed for his bottle. His face turned all shades of purple before they took him into surgery. On our way home that day we both admitted that our boy was going to be much more than the little life adjustment we anticipated.

Although the hernia operation seemed to take care of his pain, it was increasingly obvious that Derek was destined to cry. And cry he did. He didn't sleep well in his crib. He constantly wanted to be held and his insatiable appetite was difficult to satisfy. I read book after book to figure out what was wrong. Then I stumbled upon one that defined Derek as a "wakeful" baby. It suggested all types of parenting skills to calm him.

I spoke to Charlie and we decided to follow the author's advice. We'd work together to sooth him and agreed that it was time to divide our large bedroom. The plans were drawn and, within a couple weeks, Charlie created our room and *Derek's* nursery.

The day of the big move, we were extremely confident that Derek would accept his new surroundings. At bedtime we placed him in the crib and prayed. I spoke softly and rubbed his back until he fell asleep.

I turned quietly, tiptoed out into the hallway, walked into the living room, and sat on the couch. Two seconds later I heard him stir; a sob turned into a cry and then a scream. That night we each took turns comforting him. Jessica started the first round, then Charlie, and then me. As long as I lifted my hand slowly he'd stay asleep, but as soon as I left the room he'd wake up crying. There were nights I rubbed his back through the bars of the crib while I laid on the floor in anticipation of quiet sleep. At times the ordeal became so tedious and tiresome I wondered if he would ever be able to sleep on his own.

After weeks of crying and weeks of rubbing, I searched for an answer. I took a good look around the room and had a revelation. I grabbed the stuffed bear on his dresser, held it in one hand while I rubbed his back with the other, and waited for him to fall asleep. As he drifted off I gently put the head of the bear on his back with the balance draped at his side and slowly lifted my hand. It worked. The weight of the bear had just the right touch. The bear had a stiff neck but Derek got eight hours of sleep.

MILESTONES

Most parents believe their child is brilliant. We expect that our offspring will be the first to accomplish milestones in short order, achieve every goal, and master every baby step before all others. Charlie and I envisioned Derek being the leader of the people; it was the definition and origin of his name. However, he had a different agenda.

During one of his well-baby check-ups, I told the pediatrician that I was concerned that Derek hadn't met some of the milestones mentioned in a book I had read. The doctor assured me that he'd catch up. I left the appointment wondering whether I had placed too much emphasis on the "milestone" thing and promised myself to let it go.

Finally, at six months Derek rolled over and was able to sit up in his high chair. The next notch in the proverbial chart would be crawling.

I'd hold him in a crawling position, move his hands ahead, then push his hinny just a little. His knees moved ever so slowly ahead before I moved his hands forward again. I showed him how "mommy" did it, then repeated the routine. After weeks of coaching he developed his own technique. Instead of getting up on his hands and knees, he began moving backward and forward on his behind. He made a great dust rag for the floors, but it was a little odd.

At his next checkup I questioned the doctor about those milestones and again he told me to stop worrying.

Derek's first birthday arrived and it was time to celebrate. We invited the grandparents over for dinner and cake. He was adorable sitting in the highchair, looking excited as we sang happy birthday and lit the candle on the cake. I took videos while he tried to remove the wrapping paper from his gifts. Jessica helped her brother and showed him how to play with the toys. He loved the cake and wore it all over his face, hair, and clothes.

Charlie and I had agreed that in order to make Derek's birthday special, we wouldn't decorate the Christmas tree until "his" day was over. After the party ended and the guests were gone, we trimmed the tree.

Christmas day the entire family descended on our little house. Nana and Pop, Trudy, Charlie's grandmothers Ma and Oma, Mom and her boyfriend Chet, my sister Irene, her husband Dan, Jessica and her boyfriend all crammed into the living room while we sat around the tree opening presents.

Mom and Trudy had fun with their grandson. They sat on the floor, a few feet apart and tried passing him back and forth in an attempt to make him walk. One of them said, "Derek, you look like a drunken sailor." Everyone laughed as he stumbled with hands outstretched. It was obvious he wasn't going to get up and walk real soon and, although I appeared amused, I didn't think it was funny.

By mid-winter it became increasingly difficult for me to leave Derek's side. He wanted me near all the time. I loved cuddling, holding, and walking him around, but my back ached by the end of the day. He'd cry "up" or "that" and I'd jump to his command. If I didn't he'd tighten his entire body, grit his teeth, and clench his fists until he got what he wanted. I knew it was a mistake, but he was so cute. After all, he was the last child I'd have. I knew I wouldn't be carrying him into kindergarten and, the doctor said, he'd start walking when he was good and ready.

Finally, at sixteen months he took his first step. Freedom at last. Within a short period of time he began walking down the hallway, in the kitchen, in his room, in the living room, and in our bedroom. He walked into walls, fell into tables, and tripped on air, but he was walking. His language was still delayed but he could talk. Once he learned a word he would repeat it over and over again.

One afternoon while cleaning up around the house, I dropped something on the floor and exclaimed, "Holy shit," then continued going about my business. A few hours later Derek dropped one of his toys on the floor, looked up at me with the cutest little smile and yelled, "Holy shit." I looked down at him as he attempted to grab his toy and asked, "Derek, what did you say?" He responded as he plopped down on the floor, "Holy shit."

I thought for a moment, took his hand, and lead him to the couch. "Derek, mommy said a bad word. From now on when I drop something I am going to say holy cow. Can you do that?" He agreed, crawled off the couch, and ran off repeating, "Holy cow, holy cow." That night while we were all at the dinner table, Derek dropped his spoon from his highchair to the floor, he looked at me, looked down, and exclaimed, "Holy cow shit." Jessica, Charlie and I looked at each other for a split second and, although we knew it was probably a bad idea, we roared with laughter. Little did we realize that he would mimic anyone, at any time, from that day forward.

One night he climbed on the couch, sat in my lap, and began to blow in my ear. At first I reacted as if I were startled and he laughed uncontrollably. We continued this game for a while but it became increasingly obvious that nothing I could do or say would make him stop. I tried a variety of tactics to distract him but he was obsessed with the act of driving me crazy.

I wondered whether Derek's mimicking, lack of control, and his inability to put sentences together were somehow connected. Again, I spoke to his doctor. As usual, he reminded me that each child develops differently. I insisted something was wrong but he disagreed. He told me, "Derek will be fine."

***

During the first couple years of Derek's life I was very fortunate to be able to work at the real estate agency around the corner from my mother and grandparents. Although Mom did most of the running around, Nana was the one who held Derek and coddled him until he fell asleep. They loved having him there and his attachment to Nana became extraordinary. He brought life into their house and I enjoyed being able to run over there during lunch to take him for a walk. I considered myself fortunate to be able to spend time with him during the work day.

After my two year stretch of good luck, the economy bottomed out. Real estate sales were going nowhere. We needed more income for the household and I had come to the realization that my situation was soon to end. Working full time meant we'd have to find a daycare provider for Derek. Jessica was great with him but she was a teenager with a social life. Mom was great for a few hours but I couldn't ask her to watch him all day. Reluctantly, I started looking. Finding employment was difficult, but finding a daycare provider was easier than I thought it would be. Suzette lived down the street next to the elementary school. She had a fenced yard and cared for quite a few boys. Teachers brought their children there and I felt very confident that it would be a good fit for Derek. I hoped that socializing with other boys his age would help him excel in areas he had difficulty with.

After an exhaustive search I was hired by a law firm about a half an hour away. I knew taking the job was a sound financial decision, but I feared the emotional toll it would have on the family.

The night before I was scheduled to start work I strategically planned my morning. I picked out my clothes, ironed them, and hung them on the bedroom door. I placed Derek's clothes on his changing table, packed everything but food in his diaper bag, and brought his car seat inside. I'd take my morning shower, blow dry my hair and have my coffee before he stirred. Then I'd feed him, get him dressed, and snap him in the car seat. I'd have enough time to quickly get ready, grab his food and diaper bag, and head out the door.

I hardly slept that night, considering all variations of my plan but, needless to say, it didn't work. He woke before I got in the shower, started crying before I began to dry my hair, fussed when I placed his breakfast in front of him, and fought to get dressed. By the time I strapped him into the car seat I was a wreck. I dropped him off at day care and drove frantically down the road only to get stuck behind a slow moving log truck. I screamed at an elderly man who couldn't find his gas petal at a green light. Gliding through stop signs, I made it to the office on time.

CONSEQUENCES

After months on the job our family began to get used to the routine. Derek seemed to fit in at daycare, Jessica was getting older and more independent, and Charlie and I were thankful for the added income. I called Suzette just about every day to get her feedback. A few times she mentioned her concerns about Derek's difficulty balancing and delayed speech.

"Suzette, I can't tell you how many times I've talked to his doctor. He keeps telling me Derek will catch up. Maybe I've been coddling him too much."

One afternoon she called to tell me that the school was screening three year olds and reiterated her concern. Admittedly, I was hesitant, but called to schedule Derek's testing. I wanted to believe that the doctors were right, that he would catch up on his own, but in my heart, I knew better.

A couple of weeks after the screening the school's report was delivered by mail. With a sense of panic, I opened the envelope and began to read the test scores. The long and short of it was that Derek was delayed eighteen months in motor coordination, language, and comprehension. I held my breath and felt my stomach tighten as I scanned down to the recommendation. I tried to keep my emotions in check but, as I read, tears flowed down my cheeks. It was determined that, in order for him to catch up to children his age, he would have to attend a pre-school and receive occupational, physical and speech therapy.

I was devastated. What happened to learning at his own pace? Is special education, at the age of 3, fine? Perhaps my concern about the milestone chart wasn't ill placed. Could it be that the doctor was clueless? No matter what the answer, Derek was scheduled to begin pre-school in September.

In the meantime I focused on my favorite season—summer. Vacationers began their descent on the Catskills and the sound of motorcycles making their way down our windy road sung a melodic tune. Restaurants were busy with customers from New York City and

New Jersey who craved a good meal. They stood in long lines waiting for their chance to ride down the Esopus on a tube, camped at the state park in Woodland Valley, or road their bicycles through our mountainous terrain.

Jessica got a job working at a tubing company. She had money, a boyfriend with a car, and the independence she craved. But we had a problem. She had become extremely argumentative and the consummate drama queen. Disagreements erupted into full blown battles. We'd scream at each other, then she'd bolt out the door. I suppose I could have blamed her bad behavior on hormones alone, but it was much more than that.

Eleven years before I met Charlie, I left Jessica's dad. I did all I could to juggle the responsibility of being Jessica's only parent but, I could hardly pay for rent, daycare, or a healthy meal. So, when a friend invited me to check out Las Vegas, I jumped at the chance.

Vegas gave me options I didn't have in New York. The pay was great, apartments were cheap, and there were certified pre-schools open 24/7. Instead of a one bedroom apartment, there were two. We no longer ate macaroni and cheese for dinner, but went to Cesar's Palace for the buffet. Life wasn't always easy. I switched jobs a few times, overdrew my checking account, didn't have the means to do whatever we wanted, but Jessica and I were together. We were more than a mom and daughter team, we were best friends.

Four years after our move out west I fell in love with a guy who promised stability, marriage, and a chance to be a stay-at-home mom. We left Vegas behind and moved to a house in Albuquerque. I became class mom and taught Jessica how to ride a two wheeler. We danced to Michael Jackson's new releases in the afternoons and walked with friends in the snow. Then, one spring evening, I was told I was "too good" for the guy, he didn't deserve me, he needed out. Within a week he was gone. I had no means of support, lived in a house I couldn't afford, and my paralegal job in Nevada was filled. I didn't want to go back to New York, but when my grandparents offered to give us a place to stay I agreed to move back. It felt demoralizing, but we needed the welcoming arms of family.

It didn't take long for me to find a job, but the apartment search was horrible. It took six months before I found a cottage five miles from my grandparents. After renting for a couple of years, I arranged for a mortgage and had a house built less than a mile from Jessica's middle school. We had a home for the two of us in the Catskills.

Nine months later I met Charlie and Jessica was less than impressed. One night, after an argument, she told me that she hated him.

"Mom, he's going to ruin our relationship. You love him more than you love me."

I didn't know what to say. She was my little girl, my buddy, and I didn't want to fail her again, but I loved Charlie and didn't want to lose him.

"Jess, I love you so much. Please, give him a chance. Nothing will change my love for you."

She didn't care, she wanted her mom.

Months later, when Charlie and I sat her down and told her we were going to get married, she masked her sadness.

When we told her I was pregnant she seemed to be a bit more acceptant of our marriage and looked forward to the birth of a sister or brother. Jessica embraced Derek as though he was her own. Unfortunately, as their relationship grew deeper, the connection between Jessica and I deteriorated. We fought often and it took a lot of work to resolve each issue.

One afternoon, Jessica came home with her boyfriend walking behind her. I knew something was up. They seemed curiously tense.

"What's up guys?"

"Mom, we need to talk to you."

"Okay, shoot."

"Mom, I'm pregnant."

My heart sank. I felt as though I was gasping for air. I asked what they were going to do. "Jessica, you're too young. How are you going to raise a child?"

"You raised me all alone and you did it. Now I'm going to do it."

I tried to talk to them, to convince them that there were alternatives, but they had made up their minds.

"Jessica, I didn't do it well. It wasn't easy. Where are you going to live?"

They had it all figured out. They had friends up north and would stay with them until they found a place of their own.

I didn't hesitate to react. I thought they were crazy and I was afraid for them, for me, and for our family. They weren't prepared. Life was going to be tough. This was not part of my plan. Jessica wanted me to embrace their decision, to say that everything would be all right, but I couldn't.

I asked them to reconsider, but they were determined to have the baby. Jessica left home hysterical while I stood crying in the kitchen. My girl was gone. About a month later they were married in my grandparents' backyard and moved into an apartment seven miles away. I didn't expect life to throw me this curve and it took a long time for my emotions to calm. The baby was due around the first of the year.

I needed an escape and Charlie suggested we take Derek camping. Acadia, Maine was one of our favorite places and the focus of our vacation. We planned our getaway with Derek's short attention span in mind. Our first stop would be somewhere along the coast.

It was cool and breezy at the beach. We walked close to the water's edge and sat to watch the waves break along the shore. Then we took our shoes off and showed Derek how to wiggle his toes in the sand. He seemed to enjoy the feeling but had his sight on the waves. Without warning he bolted up and ran toward the water. Charlie and I jumped up and grabbed him as the wave reached his toes. There we stood, the three of us holding hands, staring at the water, as the sand snuggled our feet.

We made it to the campsite as planned, set up the tent and bedding, then took a ride into town for supplies. That night Charlie cooked lobster on the campfire. We roasted marshmallows and Derek fell asleep in my arms in front of the fire.

That morning we woke to the sound of thunder and a light rain bouncing off the tent. By lunchtime the rain intensified. We watched as the clouds blew to the east. Each time a hint of sun showed through the trees we ventured out. The weather pattern hovered over us for three days. The tent became so wet that the droplets of water leaking through soaked our sleeping bags. We grew weary. Our perfectly planned trip was turning into a disaster.

Derek had difficulty negotiating in the mud. He invariably searched out puddles to step in, then slipped and fell. By the fourth day the rain began to wear on our nerves. Charlie got annoyed with the mess around the campsite. He'd yell at Derek to wipe his feet before going in the tent and I'd get mad at Charlie.

Derek cried and I did my best to calm him.

"Honey, wipe your feet before you go into the tent."

"Okay."

"Please be careful. You have to watch where you're going."

"Okay, Mommy."

"Look out for the tree roots and rocks so you don't fall."

"Okay, I'll look."

He'd be good for the next half hour but then he'd forget. The rain continued to fall and our frustration grew. After spending more time doing laundry than sightseeing and hiking, we decided to pack it up. The sun came out on our way home. Maybe it was an omen. We decided to skip camping for a while. Maybe we'll rent a cabin.

LESSONS LEARNED

Summer days were getting shorter. September had arrived and Derek was scheduled to start pre-school for special needs kids. A week or so before, his teacher and I had a telephone conference to go over his "plan" and to prepare me for the events to come. She told me that given Derek's delays, he might have difficulty transitioning from daycare to pre-school and as long as I didn't over react he'd be fine.

Fine. There's that word again. I prayed that one day I'd wake up and Derek would be fine. In fact, I convinced myself that would happen. In the meantime, I had to make the transition as stress-free as possible.

The first day of school we went through our normal routine. While I got dressed, Charlie left for work. Derek had breakfast while I fixed my hair and put on makeup. I got him washed, dressed, and his shoes tied.

I nervously paced through the house anticipating the arrival of the bus while Derek played in the living room. When the bus pulled in the driveway, I could feel my entire body tense. I grabbed his book bag, called him to the door, took his hand, and led him down the steps. His aide came out to greet us and to my surprise Derek didn't seem worried at all. In fact, he was happy to meet his new friend.

I gave him a big hug and kiss before the aide helped him on the bus and as it pulled out of the driveway, waved goodbye.

I cried as I drove down the road and did all I could to gain my composure before getting to the office. As promised, I got a call from the teacher that afternoon. Derek, apparently, did better with the transition than I did.

She reminded me to check his home book every night and to call her if I had any questions. That night Charlie and I read the first entry. "Derek is a very sweet boy. He likes his classmates and teachers so much he can hardly contain himself, but ..."

There's always a "but."

"... he hugs with such force we have to pry him off. We'll have to work on personal space and try to help him understand his strength."

Patricia Stroh

I suppose I underestimated his strength, never giving thought to the pain one might endure because of his exuberant hugs.

Most mornings the bus arrived a few minutes before I had to leave for work. When it ran late, I'd have to speed down the highway to get to the office on time. Contemplating a late arrival to work, road rage became my release.

One morning while waiting for the bus, Derek began spinning around like a whirling dervish.

"Derek, stop it. You're going to fall!"

He ignored me and continued to turn, kicking up sand and gravel.

"Derek, I said stop."

He made an abrupt stop, lost his balance and fell. As I picked him up I saw a pretty good sized gash on his knee.

I took his hand and walked him quickly toward the door.

"I told you to stop."

He apologized through the tears.

"You have to listen to me."

I quickly cleaned the cut and dirt then placed a bandage on his knee. As I hurried him out of the house and down the stairs, I missed a step and fell to the ground. My stockings were ripped, my knee was cut and blood was dripping down my leg.

Derek looked at me, shook his head and said, "You have to be more careful."

The bus showed up minutes later. I handed him over to the aide and left for work. As I sped down the road, I couldn't help but laugh. No doubt, at some point, Derek's teacher would make an entry about his sense of humor.

During the first semester, Charlie and I read the home book together. I, the consummate optimist, held onto every sign of improvement while Charlie, the realist, didn't share my enthusiasm.

"The fact that Derek is becoming more aware of his personal space is encouraging, don't you think?"

"Yeah, Pat, it's encouraging, but don't get too excited."

"Why? Don't you think this is great news?

"It's good news, but he has a long way to go."

Well, he might be the realist in the family, but I had faith and would do everything in my power to prove him wrong.

FAMILY DYNAMICS

Each winter I pulled the same holiday decorations from the attic and found clever new ways to display them. As usual, the Christmas tree rested in a bucket outside until after Derek's birthday dinner and cake.

His fourth birthday was Thursday, December 23, 1993. That afternoon, my boss handed out bonuses, closed the office, then took us for a holiday lunch consisting of French cuisine and, of course, French wine. It was my first holiday lunch with the firm and I promised myself to be good, but the wine went down too easily. I'm sure I made a fool of myself but managed to drive home unscathed.

As soon as I walked in the door I opened the mail and found a card from my old friend Ray from England. We hadn't talked in a while and a long distance call wasn't cheap, but it was two days before Christmas and I wanted to say hello. I rambled on about Jessica's pregnancy, her husband, Derek's difficulties, politics, and marriage. And, after an exhausting conversation of laughter and tears we said goodbye and I fell asleep.

I woke minutes before Charlie and Derek walked in the door, quickly set the table, and got dinner going. I rushed around for a half hour before Jessica, her husband, and the rest of the family showed up. After dinner and birthday cake, Derek opened his presents. We were very fortunate to have family members to celebrate our son's birthday but I, for one, hoped they didn't linger too long.

Ever since Jessica was a little girl she had the pleasure of placing the angel on top of the decorated tree. It was sad to know that she wouldn't be with us Christmas Eve, but she had her own tree to decorate and it was Derek's turn. After the lights, tinsel, and ornaments were strategically hung on the branches, Charlie lifted him high above the tree top and I directed the placement of the angel.

After admiring our work of art I put my plan in motion, placed cookies and eggnog out for Santa, and gave Derek his new pair of holiday pajamas. A little while after tucking him in for the night, I motioned to Charlie to follow me to the deck, grabbed a few bells, and said, "When I count to three and ring the bells, would you yell on Dancer, on Prancer?"

Charlie, in a deep Santa voice and jokingly shaking his extremely fit belly, yelled, "On Dancer, on Prancer, on Comet, on Vixon." I rang the sleigh bells and stomped my feet. Later, as soon as we were sure Derek had fallen fast asleep, we placed the presents under the tree, ate the cookies, drank the eggnog, shut down the lights and went to bed.

The next morning I heard Derek wake up and sneak through the hallway. When he turned into the living room he let out a gasp and then ran toward our bedroom.

"Shhh, Charlie, let's make believe we're asleep."

I closed my eyes and waited. Derek stood next to my bedside and whispered in my ear,

"Mommy, Santa Claus was here."

"He was? How do you know?"

He replied quietly, "I looked."

"Well, as soon as Daddy gets up we'll open presents."

I turned to Charlie and said, "Get up, it's time."

We sat bleary eyed hovering over our coffee while Derek methodically ripped off bows and wrapping paper. In unison we gasped with excitement as each toy was revealed. After Charlie and I exchanged gifts, we began to prepare for company.

Weeks before Christmas I anguished about the dinner table. The plates and glasses had to reflect the same holiday scene. The candlesticks had to be tastefully decorated and the serving bowls had to match. But, most of all, the seating arrangements had be perfect.

I lost sleep at night wondering how to fit twelve people around a table made for six. It had to accommodate: Nana in her wheel chair; Pop, who had become unsteady on his feet with worsening Alzheimer's; a very pregnant Jessica with a less than jovial husband; my sister Irene and her husband Danny, who was in remission from a bone marrow transplant; my mother and her friend Chet; Trudy, Charlie, Derek, and me.

Charlie saved the day. He took a large piece of plywood from his shop and taped it to our small table. It gave me just enough space for the entire family. After the table was set and the centerpiece in place, I lit the candles, stepped back and marveled.

My lavishly decorated plywood table was a hit, but it certainly wasn't worth the sleepless nights. After all, the family came to celebrate the day and to watch Derek's expression as he opened each gift. They squished themselves into our living room and handed him neatly wrapped packages, munched on appetizers and drank eggnog while I worked in the kitchen. After the food was done, I called the clan to the table and what took hours to prepare took half an hour to eat.

The conversation around the table consisted of Pop continually asking where he was, Mom repeatedly telling stories of Chet's remarkable ability to befriend everyone, Jessica speaking about her physical condition, and Irene and Danny suggesting parenting skills. In the meantime, Derek made a mess of himself using his hands, rather than his fork, while Nana and Trudy, the two diabetics, slugged down their eggnog.

Not long after coffee, everyone but Jessica and her husband left for home. She was feeling sick and, though she thought she was all grown up and ready for motherhood, she needed me. I tried to convince her that everything would be fine, but it didn't work.

I could see fear in her eyes when they stopped by New Year's Eve day. She was horribly bloated and pale. When she told me that she hadn't slept all night and was in a great deal of pain, I made her call the doctor. As I expected, he instructed them to go straight to Benedictine Hospital.

Not long after they left, Charlie got home from work. He stayed with Derek and I drove to Kingston where I'd wait with Jessica's in-laws. Every once in a while one of the nurses would peek in the waiting room to give us an update. After midnight we were told she was being moved to the delivery room for a C-section. Jessica couldn't hold on any longer and the baby needed to be born. Within a half hour her husband walked through the waiting room door with eyes wide open and a huge smile on his face. It's a girl! Nicole had arrived.

I had been so worried about Jessica having a child at such a young age but, there she was. How could I or anyone turn their backs on such a beautiful creature? While I held her tiny little hands in mine and stroked the top of her head, it seemed natural to be her grandma.

Within a month or so I began feeling a sense of relief. Jessica was developing good parenting skills, continued her education, planned to graduate high school with her class, and attend college. Derek's speech was improving. He seemed comfortable walking down stairs, and his handwriting was almost legible.

As I began to feel a bit of normalcy in my life, my mother started to give signs of weariness. She was having a hard time taking care of my grandparents. Pop never graduated high school but was extremely well read. He invested well in the stock market, knew quite a bit about foreign affairs, and had very definite political convictions. He was my favorite person to debate. Unfortunately, Alzheimer's was taking everything away. He was angry, didn't know the old lady who sat at the dinner table with him, and was unable to take care of his personal needs.

On the other hand, Nana's mind was still focused, but her health was deteriorating. She had fallen years before and broke her hip. Diabetes prevented proper healing and she never walked again.

One afternoon my mother sat me down and told me that it was time for them to go to a nursing home. Pop had no idea where he was or where he was going, but Nana did. She called me and asked me to stop by after work. When Derek and I walked in the door we found her sitting in her chair, crying.

Derek climbed on her lap while I sat on the floor next to her chair. She asked me to talk to my mom and to tell her she didn't want to go. Derek wiped her tears and hugged her tight. I didn't know what to say. I had no control. The decision wasn't mine. I told her how much I loved her and that I didn't want her to go but, within a couple of weeks, they were both moved to Margaretville Nursing Home.

My grandparents were the most understanding, considerate and steadfast figures in my life and I felt as if the core of my strength was fractured that day.

As the school year came to an end, the district scheduled a meeting to determine Derek's Individualized Education Program, IEP. I was sure that the teacher's report would be gleaming. Instead, she threw me curve by recommending continued, consistent education during summer school. In fact, she would insist that he become a 12 month student.

During the meeting Charlie and I sat in a cramped, hot, classroom, surrounded by teachers and therapists. The Special Education Coordinator sat at the head of the table with Derek's file and a school budget in hand. We each spoke of our hopes for Derek and pondered how he could obtain the best possible education available. By the end of the meeting we begrudgingly agreed to send him to BOCES for summer school, then return to Sophie Finn for another year. After signing the necessary documents to set the plan in motion, we thanked everyone for their effort, got up and left the room.

Charlie took my hand as we walked down the steps. With teeth clenched and a stream of tears flowing down my cheeks, I let out a scream. The drive home was intense. I tried my best to bring up the positive aspects of the meeting and Charlie did his best to make me understand the realistic version. I hated reality and, by the time we pulled in the driveway, convinced myself that this was just another hurdle I needed to climb.

DIAGNOSIS #1

After Labor Day, Derek returned to Sophie Finn. Each of his teachers and therapists continued to be encouraging. We read his home book every afternoon and worked to adjust behaviors and patterns.

Toward the end of the first semester I received a call from the school. The physical therapist wanted to meet with me to discuss Derek's progress. I saw changes in his ability to balance and wondered whether the therapist would be showing me strengthening exercises to use at home.

Before going to the meeting, I stopped in Derek's class to say a quick hello, then went upstairs to the therapist's room. He greeted me at the door, asked me to have a seat, and began talking to me as though he had prepared a speech for the occasion.

"Mrs. Stroh, thank you for meeting with me today."

"Thanks for helping my son, I replied."

"First of all, I have to tell you that Derek is a very sweet and loving child. I enjoy working with him."

"Thanks. I kind of like him, too."

"He has made a lot of progress during the year, *but ...*"

There's that word again.

"… Derek has reached a plateau. I've tried everything possible but I never feel it's enough. I'd like to suggest that you take him to a pediatric neurologist for evaluation."

As he spoke, I held my breath, then asked, "Why didn't the doctors suggest this? They told me he'd get over this."

"I don't know. Again, he's a great kid and he works very hard, but there is something holding him back. I really think he needs to be seen by a neurologist."

He said that Derek's muscles were tight and I had to agree. There was a clumsiness to his gate that wasn't improving with exercise, which I couldn't dispute.

As I left his office I thought of stopping by the class again, but I couldn't. I felt a sense of panic as I rushed past the room, ran down the steps to the parking lot, and got in the car. As I sat quietly, taking one huge breath, I looked across the road to the entrance of the hospital where Derek was born. Then, with eyes wide open and stomach cramped, I held in a scream.

As soon as Charlie got home from work I told him what happened. We sat at the kitchen table and looked over the recommendation together. It was difficult to absorb emotionally, but intellectually we realized that perhaps this event might lead us to the answers we looked for since Derek's birth.

The next morning I scheduled an appointment with a pediatric neurologist in Westchester. Charlie had a deadline at work and wouldn't be able to go, but I wanted to get it over with.

As I drove down the thruway the day of the appointment, I did all I could to distract myself from any sense of reality. Derek and I sang silly songs from Kingston to Westchester. I made light of the day and tried to keep my attention focused on anything pleasant. The weather was nice, the traffic was light, and it really didn't matter what the doctor said. My son was the most precious thing in my universe and that is how it was going to stay.

I pulled into the parking lot just minutes before his appointment. Seconds after walking through the door a nurse called us into the office. The doctor sat at her desk with a file entitled "Derek Stroh, DOB: 12/23/89." We introduced ourselves and took our appointed seats. While reading the file, she asked me questions about my pregnancy, Derek's birth, and any pertinent information regarding his difficulties. Then she got up from her desk and said, "Derek, I would like you to walk across the room for me, please."

He walked.

"Now, can you hop on one leg?"

His balance was off, he couldn't do it.

As the doctor checked his reflexes and felt his muscle tone, she spoke to him in order to evaluate his speech patterns.

After a five minute examination she said, "Mrs. Stroh, your son has a mild case of Spastic *Diplegic Cerebral Palsy.*"

The feeling of instant panic rushed through my brain. What does that mean? The vision of Derek sitting in a wheel chair, unable to talk, unable to eat, flashed before my eyes.

Obviously, she was used to seeing this reaction and quickly responded,

"Do you see Derek's difficulties now?"

"Yes."

"That is the worst he will ever be. With proper therapy he'll improve."

As my hands began to shake, and voice quiver, I shook my head, "Okay."

Then she said, "Let's get an MRI of his brain and we'll see what's going on in there."

She wrote a prescription and sent us on our way.

Before leaving the building I began counting all of our visits to doctors during the past few years of hell, trying to come to terms with Derek's disabilities. We trusted the professional opinions of doctors all these years and it took ten minutes to come up with a diagnosis of Cerebral Palsy. As I drove onto the thruway toward home, I started to cry. Derek reached over, patted my arm and said, "It's okay, mommy."

I looked at him, shook my head and said, "I know, Derek, everything will be *fine*. I love you."

I drove directly to my mother's house, walked in the door, and broke down. Somehow growing out of it just didn't seem to work anymore.

After Derek's fifth birthday and the Christmas holidays were behind us, I scheduled his MRI. The receptionist explained that because of his age he would have to take pre-testing medicine to put him to sleep. The morning of the MRI we arrived half an hour early, checked in at the front desk, and waited. The technician brought us a cup of liquid medication and told Charlie and me that the sooner Derek drank it the quicker we could get the testing done. With a little reasoning and a lot of bribery, Derek drank the concoction.

We waited for the medicine to take effect, constantly checking my watch for the time. Within a half hour, we knew we were in trouble. Instead of falling asleep he seemed to be drunk; slurring his words, rolling his eyes, and losing his balance.

The technician checked in on us and said that he couldn't give him more medication and, if it didn't work soon, Derek would have to go to a hospital for the MRI. Charlie and I took turns carrying him over our shoulders, walking, rocking, and trying to calm our inebriated boy.

Finally, he seemed to become a little drowsy and the tech decided to give it a try. It didn't work. As soon as we placed him on the table he woke up and we left with a referral to a pediatric neurologist at Albany Medical Center.

When we got home, I called Albany and was told that Derek would have to be seen by their neurologist before the MRI could be scheduled. The day of the initial examination Charlie went to work and I drove to Albany.

Again, I answered the doctor's questions about my pregnancy, Derek's birth and his difficulties. He instructed Derek to walk down the hallway and back, stand on one foot, and attempt to hop. After checking his speech patterns, I was handed a prescription for the MRI and directed to make an appointment.

A few weeks later we headed back up to Albany for the test. Charlie and I tried to make light of the situation by telling jokes and making Derek laugh along the way. When we arrived at the hospital we were taken to the radiology department where he was given a strong dose of sedation. We waited a while, the nurse checked in on him and said, "Just a *little* longer." A little more time became hours and Derek still hadn't settled enough to stay still. The nurse said, "I don't know what's going on. He has enough medicine in him to knock out a small horse!" We walked out of the hospital with Derek slung over Charlie's shoulder. No answers today.

Charlie and I talked about another attempt and decided to wait a while. After all, Derek was the worst he was going to be and he'd continue to get the same therapy without a confirmation. Besides, it was just too painful to watch.

WATER WORKS

Derek loved water. He'd splash while bathing until the water was cold enough to turn his skin blue. Bath time became quite the production and, though I knew what the end result would be, I set the stage for the inevitable.

I filled the tub with warm water, set the soap, shampoo and conditioner and announced, "Derek, it's bath time." Without hesitation he emerged from his room, entered the bathroom and began preparing for this pleasurable event.

I closed the door behind me and yelled, "Don't make a mess this time, okay?"

Within a minute or so, I could hear the slight movement of water. It escalated to the sound of a gentle tide. The tide grew louder as it was sent crashing against the surf wall.

"Derek, slowdown in there. You're going to make a mess." No response.

I knocked on the door. "Derek, is everything all right in there? You're not getting water on the floor are you?"

"No, mommy."

As I walked toward the kitchen I heard a wave, then the squeak of his body against the less than full fiberglass unit. I turned around, walked swiftly through the hall, knocked on the door and walked in. There he was, on his stomach, arms outstretched in an empty tub. The floor drenched with water.

"Get out, Derek. What did I tell you? No water on the floor."

Charlie heard the commotion and came to the bathroom door. "What are you doing? Didn't mom tell you to keep the water in the tub? Get out and dry off."

Derek grabbed a towel and ran back into his room, apologizing once again for the mess. Charlie and I used towels to sop the water, threw them in the washing machine and used a mop for the rest.

When my grandparents gave us their pool I promised that we'd put it to good use. However, Charlie was dead set against it, wanting nothing to do with the installation or the care. He said, "If you want that fucking pool, put it up yourself!"

I took the dare and made a few calls. My mother and friend, Liz, agreed to help me. Mom had taken the pool down and was sure she could figure how to put it up. After all, how difficult could it be? So, we scheduled our little project for the following Saturday.

That morning, after Charlie left for work, I began collecting all the tools we needed, including a 2"x 4" for leveling the dirt. I called Derek out to help pick up pebbles, sticks, or clumps of grass while I shoveled.

"Derek, how about helping me clear some of the stuff on the ground for the pool?"

"I don't know how."

"All you have to do is pick up the tiny stones and the twigs and throw them in the woods, or pull up some grass in the circle."

He slowly picked up a few pebbles and sticks, threw them in the woods, then began pulling grass *one blade at a time.*

"Derek, forget it. It's okay. Go watch cartoons. I'll check on you in a little while."

Mom and Liz showed up at around 9:00 a.m. It took hours for us to remove the remaining grass, rocks and sticks. We crawled on our hands and knees using pieces of lumber to smooth the area in an attempt to make it as level as possible.

After a short break, I handed my mother a couple pieces of the wall supports.

"Mom, how do we put these together?"

She looked at them, turned them around, placed them side by side on the ground and said, "I think they go this way." She was clueless.

By 1:00 p.m. the heat of the sun was brutal. I started feeling dizzy and sick to my stomach, but continued to place the supports around in a circle. I used a screwdriver to remove dirt and widen them enough to slide the wall through while Mom and Liz put them together.

My stomach began to growl and my head pound. After losing my breakfast in the woods, I picked myself up, got a glass of water and went back to work.

"Mom, now what?" Do you have any idea how this is supposed to work?" She didn't.

If we were going to get the damn thing up before Charlie got home we needed to get our act together. It was agreed that Liz and I would hold the ends of the wall and mom would stabilize the middle. We struggled to stand it up, then attempted to roll it out as straight as possible, picked it up about an inch off the ground, and started to move it around the circle. With each step, the metal caved. Finally, after what seemed like an eternity, we got a small portion of the wall inside the circle, then the whole thing was set in place. As we tried to get the two ends to meet, Charlie pulled into the driveway.

He walked over, looked at our work, shook his head and said, "This thing isn't level. What were you thinking?"

If he knew what I was thinking my plan for Derek happily swimming in a pool would have been shot. I kept my mouth shut as he begrudgingly put the hunk of metal together; cursing and screaming.

The next day we worked on the liner and started filling the pool. As the water level rose, it was more than evident that the earth containing the sweat of our labor was less than level. But, Derek wouldn't care. He'd have a great big tub to play in without getting in trouble for letting a *little* water out.

Charlie and I learned how to regulate the filter system and took turns cleaning and shocking the pool. By the time the water and chemicals were regulated, Derek graduated pre-school and we were ready to conquer the ocean.

One of our friends told us about a great place to vacation in Virginia. Not only was First Landing a wonderful campsite a couple miles from Virginia Beach, but there were cabins for rent. While planning our adventure, Charlie and I discussed the enormity of the trip. An eight hour car ride would be too long for us to handle. We contemplated Derek fidgeting all the way and us losing our patience. So, we broke the trip up by taking the Cape May Ferry from New Jersey to Delaware, staying in Ocean City overnight, and driving to Virginia the next day.

We arrived at the campsite around noon, checked in and drove up to our cabin. It looked as though it was made for us; placed neatly along a quiet, gently sloping road. And, when we opened the door, both Charlie and I were impressed. The kitchen was a good size with all the amenities. I looked in the cabinets and found dishes, silverware, glasses, pots, pans and a coffee pot. The living room, two bedrooms, and bathroom were nicely furnished and larger than our rooms back home.

After unpacking the car we decided to check out the area. The bay was about a five minute walk from our cabin and we were anxious to see what it was like. As we approached the beach I couldn't help but notice that it seemed empty. There were a few fisherman, a couple of kids playing in the sand, and a man swimming with his dog. The view was spectacular, the sun was shining, and the water was warm.

Then, suddenly, as if someone opened a window in an insect lab, hundreds of large horse flies began their attack. Charlie and I tried to wave them away but they kept on coming. I grabbed our things, Charlie picked Derek up, and we ran through the sand toward the camp store where we were met by a few state employees. They had experienced the fly infestation since the beginning of the season and suggested that we stay away from the bay.

The next morning we packed a lunch, lots of suntan lotion, a few towels, and headed for the ocean. The salt air, the feel of sand between my toes, and the sound of crashing waves comforted me. Derek loved digging in the sand and playing catch with the waves and Charlie was the king of sandcastles.

One afternoon, after laboriously working on every detail, creating a masterpiece in the sand, Charlie called Derek to take a look. He stood over the castle, his eyes wide open, and said, "Wow! Can I step on it?" Before Charlie had a chance to respond, and with a great deal of enthusiasm, he jumped in and wiggled his toes until the creation disappeared. He looked up at Charlie and said, "Daddy, make another one." That afternoon I chased after him protecting every sandcastle on the beach from impending doom.

Just before the vacation came to an end, Derek befriended a patient young girl who was willing to build a sandcastle with him. As they began to create their masterpiece, I wondered whether the act of building one would end his path of destruction. Perhaps he would treasure his work and admire it until the waves washed it away.

Derek was in charge of filling his bucket with sand while his friend built the structure. They collected shells to decorate their work of art, then dug a moat to protect it from the waves. We watched as they put the finishing touches on their creation, then got up from our beach blanket to admire their work and his little friend's patience. Within seconds, Derek jumped into the center of the sandcastle, wiggled his toes, then turned toward to ocean and ran for a wave.

GAINS AND LOSSES

The week after our Virginia vacation Charlie and I were back to work and Derek was back at BOCES. His education piece was repetitive but the physical therapy was spot on. He received swimming lessons at the local YMCA and became the school's *fish*.

In the meantime, our pool became the center of our social network. Kids who never came to play before showed up with their parents for a dip and Jessica brought Nicole to the house more often.

One night, before summer's end, Charlie and I sat on the deck with our exhausted little *fish* and looked down on the glistening water in the pool.

"Pat, I think I'm going to take the pool down for the winter and put it up right next year."

"Really?"

"Yeah, it was a good idea."

Derek started kindergarten a couple days after Labor Day. We were thrilled that he was placed in a regular class with *normal* kids and that his teacher was a good natured, loving woman who enjoyed her job. She was enthusiastic and wore a smile every time I stopped in to say hello. She wrote words of encouragement and support and placed happy face and star stickers on each page of his home book.

If it wasn't for the crazy bus schedule, everything about Derek's education plan was a perfect fit.

Unfortunately, I had less time to get to the office and Derek didn't make that part of my morning easier. I'd lose my temper when he didn't get dressed in time. He was old enough to put it together without me constantly nagging him, but every morning was the same. I'd beg him to get dressed and, within a short period of time, began to panic. I'd yell, "Derek, get dressed. Come on, help me get your clothes on. When are you going to learn how to tie your shoes? Derek, hurry up, we're going to miss the bus and Mommy is going to be late."

For weeks the pattern continued. He wouldn't help, I'd yell, get him dressed, rush to meet the bus, and drive like a maniac to work.

One evening, in anticipation of the next day's insanity, I considered new strategies. Counting to ten didn't work. Threatening him didn't work and screaming made it worse for both of us. I tried to tempt him by promising little toys, stickers on the refrigerator, and pizza on Friday nights, but nothing motivated him.

Then, it came to me. I ran into his bedroom and declared, "Derek, I have a great idea."

He looked intrigued.

"We are going to have a dress race tomorrow."

"What's a dress race?"

"You'll see. Let's pick out some clothes for school."

We picked out a pair of pants, a shirt, cartoon boxers, socks and shoes, and laid them on his dresser.

"Okay, kiddo, so this is the deal. Tomorrow, after breakfast, we are going to have a race and the first person that gets dressed wins a prize."

"I like that game," he said.

"I'm glad, Derek. I hope you win."

That morning, after Charlie left for work, I set the stage placing Derek's favorite snack strategically within view, poured his cereal, walked to his bedroom, sat on the bed and whispered, "Derek, time to get up."

To my amazement he bolted up, ran into the kitchen and sat at the table.

"When's the dress race?"

"As soon as you finish your cereal."

"Okay."

Before I had a chance to drink my coffee he was finished eating. He quickly drank his glass of milk and asked, "Can we start the race?"

"Sure, let's go."

I led him to his room and explained that, no matter what, the first person to get dressed would win the prize. Then, I hurriedly rushed through the hallway toward my bedroom and yelled, "As soon as you're ready to start the race say *ready set go*." As I methodically moved my clothes from the dresser to the bed, I heard a flurry of activity. The little sneak started to get dressed and just as he was about finished he shouted "Ready, set, go."

I slipped my skirt on under my bathrobe, placed my shoes on the floor and pretended to have difficulty putting my pantyhose on, when he came running into the room.

"Mommy, I got dressed first."

"You did. You are fantastic; you get the prize."

Derek got on the bus that morning with an extra bag of goodies and I drove to work with a smile on my face.

While we coasted through the first month of kindergarten, my sister and her husband were anxiously awaiting the birth of their twins. Irene had a difficult time conceiving and it was nothing short of a miracle that she would have her deepest wish granted. Finally, on October 2, 1995, Michelle and Matthew were born.

Our families were complete; Irene and Danny comfortably enveloped in their new role as parents, Jessica boldly taking on the responsibilities of motherhood and marriage, Nana and Pop having settled into the nursing home, and Mom and Chet *nurturing* their relationship.

Charlie and I had a reprieve from stress and felt confident as Derek accomplished many of the goals planned for the beginning of the year.

It was a time of great relief. I felt a sense of calm with the hope that life was taking a turn toward the positive.

Then, the preverbal shit hit the fan. Jessica's marriage began falling apart. She did her best to hold everything together but, raising a child and going to college with limited income put an enormous strain on the her and the relationship. Her husband, like many young men, craved more attention than she had time to give. One day, after a huge fight, Jessica grabbed Nicole, some clothes, got in the car and drove away.

They stayed with us for a while but the situation wasn't healthy. The house was too small for the five of us and, after a month or so, Charlie and I set them up in an apartment.

Most Saturdays I drove to the nursing home to visit my grandparents. No matter what kind of pain Nana was in, she greeted Derek and me with a warm smile. She cherished the time spent with her great-grandson and made a point of rewarding him with individual bags of potato chips she horded during the week. She loved touching his thick head of blonde hair and marveled over his doe sized eyelashes.

He made her laugh and she gave him a lap to sit on. Nana always listened, had a non-judgmental personality, and embraced Derek completely.

On the other hand, Pop was difficult to spend time with. Alzheimer's disease had taken a firm grip on his mind. My once engaging, political savvy, economic wiz of a grandfather didn't know who I was. He loved the *kid* but didn't know his name. During one visit, the drool emanating from his mouth was relentless and I couldn't handle it. I gave him a quick big kiss on his forehead, said goodbye, grabbed Derek's hand and ran for the elevator.

Not long after, while my mom was visiting Irene, Danny and the kids on Long Island, I got a phone call. Pop died early that morning and they were holding his body in the hospital until Nana had a chance to say goodbye.

I jumped in the car and drove to the nursing home where I was directed to Nana's room. There she sat in her wheelchair with her hands covering her eyes, sobbing ever so gently. I walked up to her, without saying a word, put my hand on her shoulder, and placed a kiss on her head. At the direction of the nurse, I took hold of the handles on the wheelchair and started the long walk down the hall.

As I pushed the wheelchair through the doorway where Pop was laying, I couldn't help but think he looked at peace. The hospital staff had wiped away every trace of the disease that took his life. The rails to Pop's bed were lowered so that I could move Nana in as close as possible. She placed her hand on his and said, "Patti, maybe he isn't dead. Maybe he's just asleep."

I held back tears as she rubbed his arm and waited for him to wake.

I whispered, "Nana, I'm so sorry."

She looked up at me with tears streaming down her face and said, "He's really gone, isn't he?"

I shook my head, "Yes, Nana."

She moved her chair closer to the bed and asked me to help lift her. She strained to give him a final kiss and said, "Goodbye Joey, I love you."

A week later Derek celebrated his sixth birthday and Christmas arrived without much fanfare.

EVERYTHING LEADS TO THE OCEAN

The winter season tends to be economically difficult for builders in our area. It's virtually impossible to break ground or pour a foundation when the snow flies and temperatures dip below freezing.

By mid-January we had a huge accumulation of snow. The drifts were so high there was no place to put it and roofs were on the brink of collapse. Many contractors took on dangerous tasks removing snow in the blustery cold and Charlie was among them.

He did everything possible to stay employed; from snow removal, renovation, and repair. One day, while talking to Dean Gitter, the developer of Catskill Corner's in Mt. Tremper, Charlie was asked to build a prototype of a kaleidoscope designed by Charles Karadimos.

He spent hours working on the prisms, creating a whimsical box that would encase the completed project and make magic. When Dean saw the prototype, Charlie was asked to be the lead carpenter in the construction of the world's largest kaleidoscope.

By spring's end a huge staging area was erected. Everyone in town was curious to see what was behind the curtained stage. Charlie brought Derek and I on a tour of the massive structure and every once and a while we'd get a peek at the thirty-seven foot kaleidoscope as it began to take shape.

It was exciting to know that my husband was working on a structure that would be in the Guinness Book of World Records.

The crew finished building the kaleidoscope in early summer and the whole town anticipated the big reveal. National television stations and journalists planned to attend the event.

That morning, Charlie, Derek and I went to witness the unveiling. We were in awe of the press coverage. As the crowd began to gather, everyone working on the project double checked their work and fail-safes. Charlie checked inside the staging area, and the crane operator gave his equipment a second look as the media spoke to Mr. Gitter.

After all systems were checked, the curtains were removed from the staging area and the three sided, thirty-seven foot prism was revealed. Our eyes were transfixed on the boom as it was lifted and turned toward the silo. The huge hook attached to the boom swayed slightly as the anxious crowd held its breath. Once the hook was stabilized, the boom was lowered to the roof, lifted, and slowly placed on the ground. The crane operator set his sights on the prism, turned the boom, then lowered it so that the hook could attach. The prism was lifted from the stage, moved to the silo, and dangled over the roof's opening. As it was lowered into position, everyone let out a sigh of relief.

The grand opening would take place just in time for the Fourth of July and we were invited to one of the first viewings of the show. Charlie and I knew that it might be a little overwhelming for Derek, so we told him what to expect.

We arrived at Catskill Corners around 10:00 a.m. and were directed to the entrance of the kaleidoscope. I held Derek's hand while we walked through the door and the three of us found a place to lie on the floor. The doors of the silo closed, the lights lowered, and the show began.

It was a stunning show, but Derek was less than impressed. The music was so loud he began to cry. I pulled him next to me, put his head in my lap, and covered his ears, but it didn't help. My entire body tensed as I tried to calm him and prayed that the show would end. Finally, the music stopped, the movie came to an end, and the lights were turned on. Derek ran out of the World's Largest Kaleidoscope hysterically crying while Mr. Gitter and a few local dignitaries waited outside for public reaction.

That night we packed the car for our much anticipated extended weekend in Lake George with my cousins. Barbara and Hughie had scouted out housekeeping cottages on the lake years before and Briar Dell became our Fourth of July get away. It had a reputation for its family atmosphere and location. The cabins were strategically built on both sides of a slopping hill leading down to the water's edge. Little Tea Island was a short paddle from the dock and the captain of the Minnie Ha-Ha was known to give his passengers tidbits of history as the steam powered boat chugged passed.

We left the following morning for our mini vacation. Barbara and Hughie beat us there and, as usual, captured the picnic table closest to the lake.

We spent a little time bringing the suitcases to our cabin, unpacking, taking our food to the community refrigerator, and filling the cooler with wine, beer and juice boxes, before heading down to the picnic table.

Barbara and Hughie are one of our most favorite couples, and having the chance to spend time with them was very special. For the most part, they understood Derek and got a kick out of him but they were also aware of the restrictions he came with. They tried to get us to take it easy for a while, and it worked for about a half hour.

As usual, Derek wanted nothing to do with sitting quietly at the table and gently gliding into the day.

When he was younger, our Lake George vacations consisted of constantly chasing after him, picking him up when he fell, and catching him as he ran to the docks. His lack of balance made it impossible to leave alone for more than a minute or so, and what should have been a relaxing time at the lake ended up being pretty exhausting.

This year his physical therapy had begun to take hold. For the most part, he ran without falling and was able to stop himself when needed. Derek now knew how to swim and, though we were confident with his ability and happy that he would be able to join his friends, Charlie and I were destined to spend endless hours in the frosty cold lake watching over him.

"Mommy, can we go swimming?"

"Let's wait awhile. I don't want to go in until it gets warmer."

"Please, I want to go."

"We'll go in a little while."

He wasn't giving up. "Daddy, can we go swimming?"

"Come on Derek, it's too cold. Mommy told you to wait a while."

"Please?"

We had no willpower. For years we hoped that he'd be able to run and play with other kids. Now that he was able to swim with them, we couldn't deny him that pleasure. So, we gave in.

After we changed into our suits, he ran to the dock with exuberance as Charlie followed close, and I lagged behind with the towels. Derek jumped in, Charlie dove, and I stood near the stairway making believe I would follow. My two guys had a blast and I enjoyed watching every minute. It took a lot of coaxing to get him out of the water, but he eventually gave in with the promise we'd go back in after lunch.

During the afternoon the rest of the cabins filled up and families made their way to the water. As long as there were other kids swimming, we got away with merely watching him rather than jumping in.

After dinner, Charlie started a campfire. We made S'mores for the kids, popped open a bottle of wine or two, then settled into our lawn chairs. It was pretty dark by the time Derek crawled into my lap. He had an exciting day and was exhausted. I rubbed his head for a few minutes before he fell asleep.

We started the next morning at the picnic table, then moved closer to the water's edge as the sun began to warm. Before long all the kids were in the water, either on inner tubes, jumping off the dock, snorkeling, or playing Marco Polo. Derek wasn't tall enough to get in the tube on his own, or advanced enough to swim to the dock, so he spent most of this time diving underwater where he could touch the bottom. Charlie and I took turns watching him or swimming with him most of the day. Hughie fished off the dock for most of the afternoon and Barbara canoed around Tea Island until it was time for dinner.

After we ate and cleared the table, we got ready for the fireworks show on the lake. With life jackets in hand the five of us got into Hughie's boat. When he pulled away from the dock and headed toward the south side of the lake, I motioned for everyone to look up. The sky was filled with stunning, vibrant stars and I couldn't help but be mesmerized by nature's special effects.

As we approached the beach I heard test shots in the distance. Minutes later the show began with such an enormous boom that it startled everyone. Derek just about jumped out of his seat and began to cry. I put my arms around him and Charlie quickly covered his ears. Each time a firework was set off we did our best to disguise the noise and before the end of the show, he watched each burst of extraordinary color with cautious optimism and yelled, "Oh, I like that one."

When the show came to an end we headed back to Briar Dell where I put Derek to bed. Barbara, Hughie and Charlie waited for me by the dock and we spent our last night at the lake together talking and knocking down a few drinks before heading in to the cabin.

Sunday morning we packed up, said our goodbyes and headed for home. Charlie and I had to return to work the next day and Derek was scheduled for another round at BOCES summer school.

Going back to work was difficult for us. It was nice to get up a little late, spend time in the sun, and not have to rush off in the morning. We had a plan to visit Rhode Island after summer school was over, so I set my sights on that.

I had hoped there were cabins to rent near Narragansett but the state park system was different than Virginia's. While searching for private cabins and inexpensive hotels, I came across the name of a real estate agent that specialized in rental homes near Point Judith and Galilee. He had a two bedroom house on a dead end road about a mile from Scarborough Beach and convinced me, sight unseen, that it was in a great location and very affordable for our needs.

Derek made it through another stint of summer school and the three of us were looking forward to our time on the beach. Rhode Island was a mere four and a half hours from home and Derek had become accustom to car trips so it was a perfect alternative to Virginia. As we got close to our destination I felt a spiritual force driving me there. Whether it was the smell of salt in the air, or the calm of a warm breeze, I don't know.

When we pulled into the driveway and took our first glance of the house it seemed fine. Charlie and I were anxious to see what the place was like inside and, as soon as we walked in the door, I was impressed. It had a welcoming, sunny, beach cottage feel to it with two bedrooms, a nice sized living room, an eat-in kitchen, and a deck facing south. By night fall it felt like home.

The next morning we drove to Scarborough Beach where we paid a pretty hefty parking fee for being a non-resident, but we soon discovered that the price was worth it. The beach itself was expansive and well groomed. Charlie and I cautiously picked a spot next to one of the lifeguard stations to lay our blanket and towels, then took a minute to look at the scenery before Derek exclaimed,

"Let's go in."

There was a mist in the air with a thin cloud cover and the only people in the water were lifeguards getting ready for their day. Charlie wasn't ready to make the big splash and I wanted nothing more than to read a magazine in peace.

"Derek, play in the sand for a while. When it gets a little warmer Daddy will take you in."

"Please, I want to go in."

He begged for a few minutes then ran toward the water and waited for a wave to break. As soon as the surf reached his feet he turned around and ran toward the beach. He played "Catch Me If You Can" with the waves for a while before asking Charlie again.

"Daddy, can we go in now?"

"Sure, kiddo, let's go."

They ran toward the waves together, and Charlie held his hand as they got slammed by the first wave. I read for a while before Derek came rushing toward the blanket.

"Mommy, come in the water."

I got up, grabbed his hand and ran in. Charlie met us just before we were hit by a crashing wave and took Derek's other hand. The two of us lifted him as high as we could. "Wee, this is fun," he yelled.

After the waves knocked the wind out of us a couple times we all agreed to get out of the water and relax for a while.

We had lunch, then Derek and I went for a walk along the shore and collected sea glass, shells, and stones while Charlie worked on a sandcastle.

Most of our days were spent on the beach. At night we'd play mini-golf, watch a movie at the cottage, or just hang out on the deck.

One night Derek and Charlie were fooling around in the living room and came up with a game they called "bug in a rug." I'm not exactly sure how it started, but Derek slipped under the rug in the living room and Charlie pretended to catch him as he moved between the rug and the floor. Each time Charlie got close to tagging him, Derek popped out and said, "Let's do it again. Let's do it again."

We took walks through Galilee, stopping to watch the lobster boats come in, bought salt water taffy, and chased after Derek down the sidewalks. It was a wonderful place and we didn't want to leave. Before we headed home, we promised each other we'd return.

DIAGNOSIS #2

Derek made a lot of advances in kindergarten and was slated to be mainstreamed in first grade. He still had an IEP and would receive physical, speech, and occupational therapy, but he was heading in the right direction. For a change, my worries seemed to take a reprieve.

Jessica was dating a guy who was very friendly and appeared to be family oriented. They were a stunning couple with a lot of dreams and Nicole was the glue that solidified their relationship. It was because of Jessica's newfound love, a man who would protect my granddaughter, that I could continue to advocate for Derek without distraction.

I knew it wouldn't be easy for him but I had confidence that his teacher would keep him up to speed. During the first month we hardly heard from his teacher. Once in a while we'd see a note in his home book advising us of some socially unacceptable behaviors. He picked his nose in front of others, had a difficult time understanding personal space, and blew in students' ears on the lunch line. Knowing that other kids his age exhibited similar behaviors we were not particularly alarmed.

Parent-teacher conferences were scheduled about a month after school started. I felt pretty confident that Derek was doing well. Whatever contact we had with the teacher dealt with his behavior. There was hardly a mention or concern regarding his learning difficulties.

The night of the conference Charlie and I walked down the shiny buffed hallway to the classroom and waited for the teacher to call us in. As soon as we entered the room I sensed that we were not going to get a gleaming report. After the initial handshake, we were asked to sit down and were handed a packet of Derek's work. As I glanced through the pages I saw a lot of incomplete assignments.

"Mr. and Mrs. Stroh, Derek is having difficulty focusing and I have concerns about his ability to continue in this class."

My optimism took a nose dive and my survival skills kicked in. I understood the behavioral stuff was hard to deal with but I thought the educational piece was resolved. After a pretty intense discussion it was agreed that an aide would make an entry in the home book every day so we could monitor his progress. However, the teacher insisted that we consider placing him in a more *modified* class.

As the winter months approached, Nana's health continued to fail. She lost a leg to diabetes earlier in the year and was now suffering with stomach cancer. She put up a good front for everyone, but we knew she was in a tremendous amount of pain.

My grandmother was the strength of our family and we were about to lose the nucleus of our world.

I drove to the nursing home most Saturdays but it was tough. I didn't know what to do when I got there. They were dosing her up with a lot pain medication and she lost her spark. The nurses put bags of chips aside so that Derek would continue to get his treat, but it wasn't the same.

One cold afternoon Derek and I went to the nursing home for a visit. We walked into her room and saw her lying in bed with an IV in her arm. I held Derek's hand as we got closer to her bedside, leaned close, and whispered in her ear.

"Hi, Nana. It's Patty. How are you?"

She opened her eyes and looked in mine and smiled.

"I had a dream that Joey was calling me."

She was preparing to die and Pop was calling for her. It was hard to let go, to come to the realization that I was selfishly holding on because of my memories and fear of the future without her.

I whispered, "Nana, it's okay, if you need to leave us, we'll be all right. I promise."

"I love you."

The next day she told my mom that Pop wanted her with him for Christmas, and so it was. Nana passed away to be with the love of her life.

Derek was too young to understand the finality of death and believed she was still with us. Every time he got in trouble, he'd interrupt my yelling and say, "Mommy, be quiet. Nana is talking to me."

I thought he was getting pretty manipulative using the death of his great- grandmother to get out of trouble but, on the other hand, they did have a special relationship. Besides, children have better spiritual connections than adults. Who was I to tell him she wasn't reaching out?

But when Nana started interrupting his homework assignments, it got to be a bit much.

He was seriously slipping behind in school and continued to have a lot of difficulty concentrating. We had battles at home trying to teach him how to spell, but nothing seemed to work. One day, after a disappointing spelling session, I lost my patience.

"Derek, you have to sit still and think."

"I am," he growled.

"No, you aren't. Stop wiggling around."

He slammed his fist on the table, got up off the chair and ran to his room screaming, "You think I'm stupid."

For a fleeting moment I wanted to say, "No, I think I'm stupid for wasting my time." But, I didn't. He was crying, I was trembling with anger, and something had to give. My head pounded as I tried to figure out what to do. He wasn't stupid. He memorized songs that I sung to him when he was three. Why can't he spell?

In that moment I wondered, could he learn the words in rhyme?

"Derek, stop crying and come out here."

He opened the bedroom door and slowly walked down the hallway where I met him with a hug and a brand new idea.

That night we sang spelling words and within a month's time we were singing "c-o-n-s-t-i-t-u-t-i-o-n" in harmony.

The refrigerator door became a showcase for his efforts and I never tired of watching him gloat when he pulled a test out of his book bag and said, "Mommy, I got a 100. I'm smart."

Unfortunately, the school was less impressed with his progress and we were called in for a special meeting.

Parents of children with special needs always hold out hope for a miracle. They pray for the day a spark will light and the pain will melt away.

I promised myself that I would never give up. I planned rebuttals and speeches to present to the teachers in an effort to keep them on board. I went down kicking and fighting. But in the end, they won. Derek would no longer be mainstreamed and would spend a good deal of his day in a more restrictive classroom environment.

Charlie and I worked hard to give him a better sense of self-esteem, but it was difficult to get him to sit still long enough to complete his tasks.

Toward the end of the school year the teachers, counselors, and therapists scramble to test the kids in preparation for CSE meetings. Derek was up for his tri-annual report and after its completion, everyone on his team was scheduled to meet with us to plan his future.

One night before the meeting his lead teacher called to discuss his progress. We had a long conversation about Derek's behavior, his inability to focus, and the pros and cons of a one-on-one aide. Then, just before we said our goodbyes, she hesitated for a minute and said, "Pat, we might have to come to terms with the fact that Derek could be *uneducatable*."

"What?" I asked.

"Derek might be retarded."

Her statement sent me into a tailspin, bringing my emotions through a rush of anger, shock, fear, and sadness. Then, I spiraled down toward an uncontrollable rush of tears.

"My son's not retarded!"

Charlie was listening to the conversation from the living room and came to my defense as soon as he heard me cry. I hung up the phone, he wrapped his arms around me and held me tight while I sobbed uncontrollably. As I began to calm, I felt his tears.

The morning of the meeting Charlie and I were directed to a room where the team of educators, therapists, and school psychologist were waiting. We went over the report from beginning to end, discussing a few positive behaviors and a multitude of negatives. When we began to focus on his IQ the psychologist went to great lengths trying to explain that, because of Derek's inability to sit still or concentrate, it was impossible for him to get an appropriate read. The result of the testing indicated that Derek had an IQ of 74—borderline retarded.

As I tried to absorb this new information, I questioned whether the results of the testing would change if he was able to sit still. If his concentration was better, would he score higher? Did he think that Derek was incapable of learning? Was this the end of his education? No one had a definitive answer and no one was willing to hedge a bet.

Before the meeting came to an end we agreed to bring Derek to a private psychiatrist and decide how to proceed from there. Charlie and I left the building bewildered. It was the beginning of our rollercoaster ride of psychological evaluations, testing, therapy and uncertainty.

A week or so later the three of us were sitting on a couch across from the doctor, answering questions about my pregnancy, Derek's birth, and his medical history. There was no need to represent our concerns about his behavioral issues because he was exhibiting them throughout the consult. He was all over the place: unable to settle down, sit still, or answer questions and, after a while, the doctor asked if he could meet with Derek in private.

Charlie and I sat in the waiting room straining to hear the doctor's questions and, after a short period of time, he called us back. Derek was diagnosed with ADHD. We weren't advocates of medication and were not thrilled with the prospect of giving him Ritalin, but if it helped him concentrate we were willing to give it a try. He'd start with half a dose during our upcoming trip to Disney World where we could monitor his reaction and get him prepared for a full dose when he returned to school.

This was the first time Derek would be on a plane so we explained the entire process to him. The morning of the flight we gave ourselves a lot of time to drive to the airport, find a parking spot, and check in. I hadn't flown much since Jessica and I moved back to New York and Charlie had only flown once before, so we were both a little nervous. Derek, on the other hand, was anxious to get to Disney World. He wanted to get on that plane and begged to have the window seat. He didn't flinch during take-off and seemed right at home in the sky.

Half way to Florida, as we ascended high above the clouds, he tapped me in the shoulder and said,

"Mommy, I don't see her."

"What, kiddo?"

"Where is she? She's supposed to be in heaven."

I realized, he was looking for Nana.

"Oh honey, Nana is a very special angel. We'd have to fly much higher above the clouds to see her. He accepted the answer, but stared at the clouds until we started our descent.

We spent a lot of time planning the trip and figured it would be best if we got to the park early each morning to avoid lines. We'd go back to the hotel around lunch time each day, go swimming in the pool until dinner time, then return to the park at night. It turned out to be a great decision. Charlie took Derek on all kinds of thrilling rides and I took him to *It's a Small World*. They loved the water park and Derek surprised us by going down an enormous slide. Epcot Center was my favorite place. I loved watching him run through the sprinklers and fountains that came out of the pavement in timed precession. He ran through them stamping his feet, laughing and yelling in sheer joy.

Our five days at Disney went quickly and it was time to head back home. Derek was doing well on the medication so we increased his dose the weekend before he returned to class.

A week or so after vacation I returned to the school for another meeting to decide his fate in second grade. We agreed that everyone would monitor his response to the medication and, for now, he would maintain the status quo.

RESOLVE

Our friends were losing their patience with Derek and began to invite us over for *adult* time. Babysitters were hard to find. Jessica was in college, and my mother and mother-in-law were busy with lives of their own. Charlie and I came to the conclusion that our social life would be limited. Our little family would be our main focus and to hell with those who didn't approve of our parenting skills. Most of our evenings and weekends were spent in the pool, barbequing, or working in the yard.

Derek settled pretty easily into the second grade routine and began to respond positively to the assistance of the classroom aides. I noticed small advances in his school work and the therapists indicated that they were seeing improvement, too. His gait began to change slightly and his handwriting started to look a bit more refined.

Unfortunately, he continued to exhibit a lot of unacceptable behaviors. He wasn't picking up the cues that other kids had mastered years before. He had no understanding of personal space and thought it was funny to blow in classmates' ears no matter how irritating it was to them. The teachers did all they could to redirect his attention to prevent socially inappropriate behaviors, but their energy was beginning to wane.

I was having difficulty restraining him from displaying public affection. He'd hug too tightly, kiss me on the lips, and people began looking at the two of us.

Then, one night after Charlie brought Derek home from the babysitters, we were told a story that no parent wants to hear.

Pizza was Derek's favorite food and it became our Friday evening ritual. As usual, Charlie and I loaded our slices with garlic and red pepper and Derek wore his all over his face.

After taking his bath I got him got ready for bed, grabbed a book, tucked him in, and laid my head on the pillow next to him before starting to read.

The bath got him all riled up and he couldn't stay still.

"Come on Derek, settle down and stop moving."

He replied, "I'm trying, mommy."

Finally he began to calm down. I rubbed his head lightly, leaned over, and gave him a kiss.

He said, "Mommy, your breath smells like garlic. I wouldn't put my tongue in your mouth."

I was dumbfounded.

"What do you mean?"

He shrugged.

"Honey, did someone put their tongue in your mouth?

"Yup."

Then, as if I possessed a key to unlock the door, he told a story about experiences he had with his babysitter's daughter two years before. As he revealed each act I sat in horror. Kissing was just the beginning.

I calmly got up, walked into the living room and asked Charlie to follow me into Derek's bedroom. I suppose the look on my face and the quiver in my voice made it evident that I was extremely upset.

With a puzzled look on his face, Charlie followed me and sat on the bed as Derek repeated the story.

There was no doubt he was telling the truth. He had never been allowed to watch anything on TV or in the movies that would remotely suggest the feelings he experienced.

***

On the advice of the police department, we made an appointment at our doctor's office where we would meet with a detective. That morning the three of us were sitting in the office nervously anticipating the interview. The nurse called us in, took Derek to the examination room, and directed us to a room where two detectives were waiting. We repeated Derek's story and they made notes. A short while later the nurse brought Derek into the office and the police proceeded with their questioning. Again, he told the same story without deviation.

One of the officers looked at him and said, Derek, how do you know that this happened to you when you were five?"

Derek looked at him and said emphatically, "Because it was before I was six!"

We all looked at each other, shook our heads, and without another word being uttered, I got the sense that they knew he was telling the truth. Later that night we received a call from sheriff's office. They brought the girl in for questioning and she admitted the entire story.

She was heading to family court and we were heading to a psychologist. Charlie and I did everything we could to stay calm in front of Derek, but we were emotional wrecks.

We knew the sitter and her family, respected them for their community service, but couldn't comprehend this. Were we neglectful? How could we have let this happen? Why didn't we recognize signs of abuse? Was he a target because of his special needs? Was it easier for her to abuse him because his speech was delayed?

Derek was an adorable boy who still hugged me until it hurt. He'd pucker up those soft little lips and give me the most wonderful kiss and now I had to worry whether it was appropriate or not. We were tormented by our questions but decided to take the psychologist's advice. He was not going to be the abused child. We were there to protect him and until the time came that he was ready to talk about it, the story was over.

Toward the end of the school year I began working with Derek's teacher to develop a plan for third grade. We were all a bit weary of the process and not sure where he was going to fit. His teacher believed he would benefit from a smaller class and recommended that he attend a school that could accommodate this needs.

I was at my breaking point emotionally and found it difficult to dispute the recommendation. After a lengthy debate at the CSE meeting, it was decided that he would make the move and the district would hire a one-on-one aide to help with his class work and socialization.

REDIRECTED FOCUS

A few weeks later we were in Lake George. Barbara and Hughie were there a few days before us and latched onto our favorite picnic table.

We were all happy to be there. The weather forecast for the weekend was great and we looked forward to relaxing by the water. The *Woodstock* crew pulled in behind us and, as always, they brought their good nature and generosity along with them.

Charlie and I anticipated a great time. Derek's balance had improved so we weren't destined to watch him constantly. He had become quite the swimmer and although we still kept an eye on him, he spent a lot of time playing with the kids without too much supervision.

One afternoon while I was lying in the sun, Derek asked, "Mommy can I have a dollar for the soda machine?"

"Can you wait a little bit?" I replied.

I had never allowed him to go into my wallet before, but he was thirsty and I didn't want to walk up to the cabin, so I gave in.

"You do know what a dollar looks like, right?

"Yup."

"Okay, take one dollar, go directly to the machine and get yourself a soda. But, if you have a hard time, let me know and I'll help."

A little time passed before he came back.

"Mommy, that dollar didn't work, it's a bad dollar, can I go get a different one?"

"Sure, try one more dollar but that's it.

I went back to my daydreaming in the sun and didn't give the soda machine another thought.

Later that day Charlie and I talked about going into town to get a bite to eat and to bring Derek to the arcade.

After collecting our wet towels I went up to the cabin to get ready. While I put things away and grabbed a change of clothes, I checked my wallet to see how much money I had. We never brought a lot cash with us because we didn't have a lot to bring, but I could have sworn I had more than sixty dollars. I looked in my purse, my jeans, the dresser draw, but found nothing. I traced back the day wondering where I spent it and then, I remembered … Derek took soda money.

I yelled for him to come up to the cabin. "Derek, do you know what a dollar looks like?" He looked at me like I was crazy. Of course he knew what a dollar looked like. It was a rectangular, green, piece of paper with some old guys face on it. But, he had no idea what a denomination was.

"Mommy, it was a bad dollar."

"What did you do with the bad dollar?" He shrugged his shoulders and said, "I threw it in the garbage, it didn't work."

"Derek, what did you do with the second dollar?"

"That one was bad too so I threw it out, duh."

I ran up to the office and asked the owner to check the soda machine for a couple twenty dollar bills but they weren't in there. When I told him I wanted to check through the garbage he said, "Ah, you're too late, the garbage man just left."

Needless to say we didn't go out to dinner that night and Derek wasn't going into my wallet anytime soon.

The next day we packed our bags, said our goodbyes, and headed for home. Charlie and I had to return to work, Derek was scheduled for BOCES, and we had a busy summer ahead.

Jessica and Ed planned a wedding in August and, as mother of the bride, I had a lot to do. We shopped for the perfect wedding dress and all the accessories. The church, restaurant, and band were chosen and a friend agreed to take pictures.

There wasn't a great deal of time to prepare, but we all worked together and the wedding party looked radiant. Jessica was gorgeous in her gown with her blonde hair flowing down beneath the veil. Nikki was an adorable flower girl and Derek was quite the handsome ring bearer. I beamed with pride as I watched them reach the altar. Ed had an infectious smile and seemed very proud as he stood next to his bride to be.

After they took their vows an hour was spent taking pictures. I was concerned that Derek wouldn't be able to stay focused. We had just increased his medication and I wasn't sure what to expect. He held it together during the ceremony and did very well during the picture taking extravaganza, but by the time we got to the reception I noticed subtle changes in his behavior. When the music started it was more than evident that he was becoming hyper focused. He picked Nikki up like a little rag doll and twirled her around until they were both dizzy. Initially it was cute, but after a while it got to be a bit much. I had about all I could take after I watched the two of them fall to the floor.

I walked up to the dance floor, lifted them up and, as I brushed the dust from their clothes, whispered, "Derek, stop for a while and sit with me."

No reply.

"You need to calm down for a while."

He looked at me with an intensity I had never seen before and replied, "Leave me alone, I can't stop."

For the rest of the night I worried that the increased dose was too much. Even though guests at the wedding commented that Derek seemed more in control, I saw something completely different.

The next day Jessica and Ed were off on their honeymoon and I began obsessing about Derek's behavior. Should we have insisted that he get another MRI rather than fear it? Was medication the only answer? If we had solid evidence that something happened during delivery would we be in a better position to help him?

I needed answers and the only way I could get them was to request a copy of the hospital records. The three page report was hard to decipher but there were two words within it that stood out; *hematoma* and *apnea*. No one ever mentioned them to us and I wanted to know why.

I scheduled an appointment with the doctor and prayed that he'd look at the report, nod his head, and confirm that something happened to Derek when he was delivered. I wanted him to tell me whether there was a connection between his delivery and his problems. I wanted him to say that he could fix everything and that I wasn't to blame. Instead I got a pat on the back, kudos for being a great mom, and a bill.

Intellectually, I knew I wouldn't get the answers I needed, but as Derek's mom, I had to try. It took a while for me to stop obsessing about the hospital records and the reason for his problems. I had to redirect my focus. None of the answers would change what happened in the past, but I would change the future.

HOW DO YOU SPELL FAITH?

I drove Derek to his new elementary school the first day of third grade. We met his new teacher, the classroom aide, and his four classmates. Melissa Thongs had an infectious smile, was soft spoken, and appeared to be very positive. Within a very short period of time I was convinced we had made the right decision. They were happy to have Derek in their class and emoted a sense of encouragement that I had never felt before.

His one-on-one aide was hired a couple of weeks after classes began and she seemed to be a perfect match. Christina was a slender, sensitive, glowing woman who was an angel in disguise. Derek was awestruck and jumped at every chance to please her. I do believe he felt as if he was the luckiest guy in school to have her by his side. We started seeing improvement in his class work and received wonderful notes of encouragement in his home book. After the first quarter, Mrs. Thongs commented in his report card that he was "Progressing with support and does very well on the reading practice test." By the second quarter his teacher wrote, "Derek is doing very nicely in this class. He is progressing in all areas. Derek is a pleasure to have in class."

Christina worked very hard to help him with socialization and he began to develop friendships. As a matter of fact, for the first time since Derek's entry into the school system, we were receiving calls from parents asking if we could get the kids together.

Life started to seem *normal*. I spent time driving him to friends' houses and stayed until I was sure the kids were getting along. Then, I'd sneak out the door for a little private time. Grocery shopping all alone was a pleasure and at times I found myself aimlessly driving down the road with the radio blasting. At times I'd stop to watch people by the Ashokan Reservoir while basking in the warmth of the sun as it radiated through the car window. It was refreshing to experience freedom and watch Derek interact with friends.

We finally had boys running around the house, making snowmen in the front yard, or playing an occasional game. I, too, had new friends—women who knew what I was feeling and how difficult life could be. We spoke about past experiences, the school district, teachers, programs, and our relationships.

Derek's ninth birthday was particularly special. We threw him a birthday party with friends during winter break. The kids had a wonderful time playing, getting a sugar high from cake, destroying his bedroom, and running me ragged. I was exhausted by the time the kids left but this is what *normal* was supposed to feel like.

His experience at school continued to be a successful one. We got encouraging signs all of the time. Mrs. Thongs continued her positive work and Derek was thriving. She reported that he was becoming more socially appropriate and his school work was improving. By third quarter she wrote, "Derek is progressing in all academic areas. He seems to have gained a tremendous amount of self-confidence this year."

He was *close* to reaching third grade level, which was a huge step in the right direction, but we wondered whether the move to fourth grade was appropriate.

I scheduled a meeting for Charlie and me to meet with the teacher in mid-May. The afternoon of the meeting we walked into the school with a rejuvenated perspective. We spoke of advancement and attained goals without a cloud of gloom and doom. We looked to Derek's future with a regained sense of hope and mutually agreed that it would be in his best interest to give him heads up the following year. He would repeat third grade and be at grade level at the end of the year.

Very early the next morning I got a call from Jessica. She was pregnant with her second child and very close to her due date.

"Hi, Mom. Sorry for waking you up."

"What's up, I asked. Are you in labor?"

"No, she replied. My water broke and the doctor told us to head to the hospital."

"Okay, do you want to drop Nikki over?"

"Yes."

They dropped her off before heading in to Kingston and, as soon as Derek was on the school bus, I rushed Nikki in to see her mom.

Jessica and Ed had promised that she would be able to see the baby as soon as it was born and I promised to stay with her while we waited.

It was everyone's hope that Jessica wouldn't be in labor for a long time, so it made sense for us to wait for her to start contracting. I walked every square inch of the hallway with Nikki before checking back with the nurses. I took her outside to have her run off some energy, then checked back again. We watched cartoons in the waiting room for a while, then went back for a visit. But, by mid-afternoon Nikki grew anxious, tired and grumpy. The contractions hadn't started yet and we knew that the baby was going to take its time making an entrance. It was agreed that I would take Nikki back home if Ed promised to call as soon as anything happened.

They checked in a couple of times before and after dinner but by 8:00 p.m. there was no news, so I told Nikki and Derek to go to bed. Charlie and I stayed up a couple more hours and finally, at 5:30 a.m., the phone rang.

I jumped out of bed and answered it.

"Hi, Mom, it's Ed."

"Is everything okay? Did she have the baby?"

"It's a girl and she is fine, but—"

"But what," I interrupted."

"Jessica's not doing too well, the doctor made a mistake stitching her up and she's refusing to let them near her until you get here."

"I'm on my way."

I turned the bedroom light on, grabbed some clothes, told Charlie what was going on, got dressed, and ran out the door. Then I sped down Route 28 and arrived at the hospital in record time. As I rushed down the hallway I couldn't imagine what I was about to see. Her room looked like a war zone with blood splattered all over the place. In horror, I walked across the bloodied floor and focused my attention on Ed. He stood by Jess' bedside with an extremely distressed look on his face.

As soon as Jessica saw me, she began to cry, "I'm so afraid Mom."

I did all I could to stay composed but I wanted to scream at someone. I couldn't understand why she was in so much pain, why the blood was everywhere, or what the doctor had done wrong. But, without reason, I assured her that everything was going to be okay.

Ed and I stood at her bedside, held her hands, and talked her through the pain as the doctors removed the misplaced stitches and sewed her up again.

When the procedure was over Ed went outside to talk to the doctor and I kept her calm. After a while she fell asleep and I tiptoed out to find Ed. We snuck out of delivery and went to the nursery to take a peak. I got my first glimpse of our little Fayth.

Later that morning I drove home to a bustling family. Everyone wanted to know what happened and I finally got the chance to tell Nikki that she had a new baby sister. She screeched with excitement and could hardly wait to see her.

On the way back to the hospital I tried to prepare the kids so they wouldn't be upset when they first saw Jess. She looked pretty beat up when I left hours before and, based on the amount of blood lost, knew she'd need a transfusion. Nikki skipped down the hospital hallway with Derek close behind while I did my best to stay a step or two in front of them, but the kids were so excited they ran passed me and entered the room. Nikki let out a scream and Derek uttered his first *what the hell,* as I stood at the doorway in shock. No one had cleaned the room and it still looked like a war zone. I grabbed the kids and brought them into the hallway where we waited for the staff to clean the blood from the floor. When one of the nurses motioned for us to go in, the kids tiptoed, looked around, and cautiously moved toward Jessica's bedside. Nikki got a big hug from Ed and looked sadly at her mom, while Derek gave his sister a gentle kiss. We visited for a half hour and as soon as Jessica began to doze, the four of us went to the nursery to see Fayth. There was no doubt in anyone's mind that she was the cutest one there.

The next morning we went back to the hospital. Jessica had to get another transfusion and was pretty weak. She was allowed to have Fayth in her room by her side. I was amazed that the hospital rules now allowed all of us to hold the baby and was thrilled when Ed handed her to me. Charlie held her in his arms for just a few minutes before Derek said, "Hey, I want to hold her. When's my turn?"

He sat in the chair, received his new niece, rubbed her head gently, and kissed her on her forehead. With a big smile, he looked up at me with a sense of deep satisfaction.

The next day Derek went to school and told everyone in class about *his* Fayth.

Weeks later the school year came to an end and I felt as though our entire family had taken huge steps in a positive direction. We had made it through a year without constant telephone calls and conferences at the school and the teacher's fourth quarter comments read, "Derek had a terrific year! I am pleased to have had the chance to work with him and to get to know him. Have a great summer. (Placement for next year: Mrs. Thongs)."

***

That summer I met Dotty at the gym. She was about my age, had a great sense of humor, and was easy to talk to. We seemed to have parallel lives. She, too, had been married, divorced, a single mom, and remarried.

After a while we joked that we lost more weight in our jaws from talking than we did walking on the treadmill. We started meeting for lunch and for drinks after work. Then, we introduced each other to our families.

Derek was thrilled that Dotty had two grandchildren. LeeAnne was a compassionate little girl who seemed to understand Derek's behavioral issues and didn't mind that he squeezed her too hard or blew in her face. Craig was a few years younger than Derek but was a happy-go-lucky boy with learning disabilities of his own.

We spent a great deal of the summer driving the kids back and forth for play dates and, in the process, weaved friendships that would last a lifetime.

GOALS ACHIEVED

I had no hesitation or concern regarding Derek's upcoming school year. He'd be in Melissa's class and Christina would be at his side every step of the way. It was a safe haven, not only for Derek, but for Charlie and me as well.

We attended after school activities, met with parents of classmates, baked cookies for holiday baskets, and went to elementary school concerts that most parents dread. One of Derek's favorite after school event was pumpkin carving night, highlighted with a costume parade. He loved Halloween, not only for the mounds of candy he'd consume, but for the characters he became. Every year I'd create the costume of his choice. He was a *candy corn* at three, then a *bunny*, a *pumpkin head*, a *vampire*, and an a*ngry beaver*. This year he was obsessed with *Megaman*. I watched him as he took center stage with a gleaming look in his eye and a huge smile on his face. That night he *was* that character and played it to a tee.

Our holiday dinners were getting a little hectic. This year Thanksgiving was split between Charlie's family and mine. We went to Trudy's for Thanksgiving dinner. She loved to cook and we thoroughly enjoyed her creations. Derek always felt at home at her house. She was our occasional babysitter/childcare provider and always there for us when we needed someone to watch over him during school cancellations. She was the queen of treats and Derek took full advantage of it. There were times that he drove her crazy, but for the most part, they got along fabulously. Trudy and I got along very well. Not only did we both adore Charlie, but we shared a love for Chardonnay and a deep desire for travel.

It was hard to leave after dinner, but we promised to be at my Mom's house for desert. Irene and Danny had driven from Long Island and I wanted to visit with them and the kids. By the time we arrived coffee was on the table. We were stuffed, but managed to gobble down some pumpkin pie and fruit cake. The time spent together was nice, but the three of us were anxious to go home, take off our holiday clothes, and slip on a pair of lose pajamas.

As Derek's birthday approached I couldn't believe our little guy was going to be ten years old. Where did the time go? We had been through so much, but it seemed that the years just flew by. I wondered what the future would bring for him and hoped that his hard work would make a difference. My dream for him was simple: to be educated, to earn a living, to fall in love, and raise a family.

Trudy, Jessica, Nikki, and Fayth came to the house to celebrate. As usual, after dinner, cake and gifts, everyone went home and we decorated the Christmas tree. This year Danny and Irene decided to stay at home so the kids could open presents under their tree and I invited the rest of the crew over to our house.

As New Year's Eve 2000 got closer, most everyone began to panic over threats and stories of catastrophic computer glitches. Just about every news agency predicted horrific scenarios if computers were unable to make a transition from 1999 to 2000. It was reported that electricity might be lost in all major grids, that trains wouldn't run, and planes couldn't fly. Generator sales went up in anticipation of the event, but Charlie and I decided not to feed into all the hype. After all, we were campers and, if something went horribly wrong, we had our camp stove, lanterns and lots of candles.

Life as we knew it could change in a second, but we decided to stick to our plans and go to a New Year's party at Belleayre Ski Center. Jessica and Ed offered to let Derek stay with them, so we planned a night of dinner, music, and dancing with our friends.

The ski house was converted to a beautiful setting for the night. The food was delicious, the band was great, and we danced until we could hardly move. As the hours passed and the countdown got closer, I couldn't help but hope that the news reports of impending gloom were overrated.

A minute before midnight the band stopped playing and everyone stood still on the dance floor in anticipation. My mind flashed back through the year as the countdown began. Then the lead singer began counting aloud; ten, nine, eight, seven, six, five, four, three, two, and then, one! Happy New Year! Charlie and I gave each other a hug and kiss and as the band began to play *Auld Lang Syne*, the microphones were still working, and the holiday lights were glowing. We held each other tight and began to dance with the promise of a better year.

With Melissa's intuitive teaching skills and Christina's attention, Derek continued to pick up speed at school. The home book notes were encouraging and this boosted my confidence in our decision to keep him back. Melissa would call me at work if he exhibited inappropriate behaviors or had difficulty focusing on class work. Our conversations made it easier to develop cohesive responses at school and at home.

Because of everyone's hard work, Derek began to reach many of the goals in his individualized plan. And though we were pleased with his progress, we knew that as a result, the district would not agree to keep Christina on. I understood the reasoning, but I was concerned. Derek had fallen in love with her and I worried how the loss of his sidekick would affect him.

As the school year came to an end, Derek was at grade level … educationally. I prayed that he'd be able to stay in Melissa's class one more year but it wasn't in the cards. Two kids were moving on, there were no other students slated to take their place and there were rumors that the district planned to disband the class.

At his CSE meeting it was confirmed that the class would no longer be an option. Melissa was moving to another school and we had to agree on Derek's placement. With the "no child left behind" strategy, it was difficult to find a place for him to fit. Budgets were decreasing and school districts were ill prepared to handle the diversity of each child's individualized plan. Derek was stuck in the middle.

He edged his way up to grade level with a lot of help. He was brighter than the kids in with the lower functioning class, but a higher functioning class without the support of a one-on-one would be difficult.

Before the end of the meeting, and with a considerable amount of trepidation, I agreed that he should be given the chance to move upwards with his two friends. There were no alternatives and, if he was to receive the best education possible, I could only hope that with a motivated educator, Derek would continue to thrive.

When the meeting concluded Melissa and I left the room. As always, she did her best to calm my fears. We said our goodbyes, gave each other a hug, and held back our tears. The last two years had been so pleasant for me as a mom and nothing short of a miracle for my challenged little boy. I had to believe that the rest of Derek's school experience could be the same.

Charlie was getting tired of doing the same thing every summer. He was afraid we were falling into a rut and decided it was time to go on a camping vacation again. We looked at the New York map together and decided to head up to Rollins Pond near Lake Placid. I had been there when I was a teenager and had pleasant memories of the lake. So, with a new tent and camping gear, we packed up the car and headed up north.

My memory of the place was surprisingly spot on. I remembered the long drive in and the pines that stood like soldiers. The campsites were large and placed far enough apart for privacy, and were right on the lake. After we scoped out the place, we set up the tent, blew up air mattresses, and decided where each of us would sleep. Then, we took a ride around the campsite and went into town to buy food for a few days.

That night, after dinner, Charlie built us a glowing fire. We told jokes, roasted some marshmallows and star gazed for a while. Before we headed into bed Charlie noticed that the stars were disappearing under a thick pillow of clouds.

"What's the forecast," he asked.

"I think we might get a few showers," I replied.

"Maybe I should have dug a trench around the tent today."

Every camper knows that the most important part of the set-up is to dig a trench around the tent. One time, when Nana and Pop took Irene and me camping in the Finger Lakes, we had a torrential rain storm in the middle of the night. When we woke up our air mattresses were floating in a pond in the center of the tent.

Sure, Charlie and I realized we should have been more prepared, but it was too dark and too late to start digging. We'd do it in the morning.

It must have been a little after midnight when I heard thunder in the distance.

"Charlie, do you hear that?

He listened for a minute, heard a rumble, and jumped out of bed.

"What are you doing," I asked.

"I have to dig a trench."

He threw on a pair of shoes, got up, and unzipped the tent.

As the thunder got louder and the lightning lit the sky, Derek woke up frightened.

"Where's Dad?"

"He's outside digging a trench."

We listened as Charlie ran around the edges of the tent, frantically digging as fast as he could, and just as we heard him maneuver to the back of the tent, there was a loud clap of thunder and the rain began to pour. Charlie quickly finished the job, unzipped the tent and jumped in soaking wet.

Derek whispered, "Hey Dad, the next time we go camping we have to dig the trench first. Okay?"

Charlie grunted, took his clothes off, and slipped into the sleeping bag. I leaned toward Derek and whispered back, "You're right, but shush. Try to get some sleep."

The next morning the tent and half the bedding was drenched, but by nightfall everything was dry and we were in pretty good shape.

Derek was becoming a bit more independent and the last thing he wanted was for me to follow him up to the bathroom. So, I'd give him a head start and, when I saw him enter the building, I walked up and snuck around to be sure he was okay. Every once in a while he'd allow me to go up with him in the morning so he could show me the lunar moths that clung to the screen door.

This particular morning he decided he didn't want me to follow him so I waited a few minutes before heading up. When I got close to the building I saw him with his hands on the screen door and, as I got closer, I witnessed him trying to crush a moth.

I yelled, "Hey, what are you doing?"

He jumped back, "Nothing!"

"Are you trying to kill the moth?"

He turned around, passed me, and ran to the campsite screaming, "Okay, I'm stupid."

As usual, I felt bad for over reacting and followed him to the campsite where I motioned for him to sit down. Then, for the hundredth time I explained that I didn't think he was stupid but that he didn't give his actions a lot of thought.

Then I told him, "Derek, if you think you are doing something wrong, you probably are." He nodded, and told me he was sorry, we hugged, and I believed he understood.

A day or so later we were on our way home. Though I had resisted another camping trip, we had a good time. We visited a few of the Olympic arenas and watched ice skaters perform and the ski jumpers land on a practice turf. We spent a good deal of time swimming, had some fantastic campfires, and Derek never failed to remind Charlie of the "trench ordeal" each night before bed.

MUSIC TO MY EARS

Even though I knew fourth grade would be tough, I hoped that Derek would be able to hold his own. His new teacher explained that the curriculum would be more difficult than he was used to, but if he was able to keep up during the next three years, he'd be prepared to enter junior high without too many modifications.

We were heading in the direction we had worked so hard to travel and I had high hopes for the future. The first semester went by pretty quickly and his teacher commented that she was pleasantly surprised with his ability to keep up. He had the support of the classroom aide and continued with physical and speech therapy.

Derek was thrilled that he was able to join the chorus. It was a great opportunity for him to be part of a group and have additional socialization with his peers. He loved music and, of course, thought that he had the best voice in the world.

The evening of the holiday concert, Charlie and I proudly walked into the school to witness his first concert. It was nice to see the kids dressed up, excitedly running around in preparation for the big event. We met some of the teachers and staff in the hallway, talked to parents about the past few months, and what it was like to make it through an elementary school concert.

Charlie and I found a couple of seats about ten rows from the risers and anxiously awaited the chorus' entrance. Much to our dismay, the orchestra was first on the schedule and we squirmed on our elementary sized chairs while listening to the torturous *sounds of music.* The ever present screech of the violins, misplaced notes on the clarinets, and off tempo drums were bad enough to give me a headache. When the orchestra completed their final song, the audience cheered with joy.

Finally, while my back began to strain and my head began to pound, it was the chorus' turn. The sixth graders marched in first as the younger children followed and stood in place. The first note was struck and they began to sing. Derek was grinning from ear to ear, but the excitement was getting to him. I watched him squirm, sing a few notes, turn and look at one of his friends and blow in his ear. "Oh, no" I thought. "Derek, stop."

He continued a repetition of singing and blowing until he heard the notes of his favorite song. Thankfully, his attention shifted and he began to sing. When the chorus finished the song he laughed with the kids and wore an enormous smile as the audience applauded.

Derek had been subjected to many nights at our local community theater while I rehearsed for productions. He hated it when I left for Phoenicia without him and I almost always gave in to his sulking. Even though he wanted to be with me, his attention span would wane halfway through the rehearsal. After all, how many times could anyone watch the same scene over and over until we got the lines, a song, or blocking right?

So, as part of a cultural experience, my mom and I decided to take Derek and Nikki to see a *real* Broadway show for their birthdays.

We got third row, center matinee tickets to see the Sound of Music and I was psyched. The morning of the show we drove to Rhinecliff and got on the Amtrak line to Penn Station. The kids were excited to be on the train and watched out the window as a barge made its way down the Hudson. After a while, Derek began playing his Pokemon game and Nikki grabbed a book to read. Just after I sang praises of their good behavior, Derek grunted something about the game and Nikki stomped her feet. He answered the stomp by blowing in her ear and she screeched, "Stop it, Derek. Stop it." Two minutes later they repeated the cycle and I threatened them with time out.

I always experience a rush of adrenalin when I go to the city and it was obvious the kids did, too. As soon as we reached street level their hyperactivity reached a new high. It was close to Christmas and the streets were all a-buzz. The sidewalks were lined with people. Taxis were screeching to a halt and car horns were a blare. Neither of the'kids had been to the city before and they had no clue how to react. They were skipping down the sidewalk without a care in the world while I watched in a state of panic. I screamed at them to stop before they reached the end of the block, then Mom grabbed Nikki's hand and I held Derek's. At ten years of age he did not want his mother holding his hand and he dug his finger nails into my palm in protest. I held even tighter.

I was relieved to see a sign for Olive Garden. We'd get a meal fairly quick, with a price that wouldn't bankrupt us, and I'd have a chance to talk to the kids about the city and their reaction.

After lunch the kids stayed close to us without being reprimanded and we arrived at the theater in good time. As soon as we walked through the doors I was reminded of the first time Nana brought me to Broadway to see My Fair Lady. It was thrilling to be in a building where magic was created and I felt that I was the luckiest girl in the whole world. Derek and Nikki were in awe of the theater as the usher brought us to our seats. When the lights dimmed and the orchestra rose from the pit, the kids waived in excitement. And, as soon as the overture ended and the curtains opened Derek let out a gasp. I turned to look at him and saw excitement in his eyes. It was a magical event for him and he was enthralled with every move, clapping with an enormous amount of enthusiasm after every song. The cast was connected to the audience and, at one point, Derek whispered, "That guy *Max* is looking straight at me, Mom." After the last note was sung he stood up and applauded with such exuberance that *Max* not only gave Derek a little wave during curtain call but, he winked at him before the curtains closed.

I put my arm around him and whispered in his ear, "That was cool wasn't it?"

"Yeah, he waved at me, right?"

"Yes, he certainly did."

On the ride home Derek played his Gameboy and tickled Nikki whenever he had a chance. She'd screech, he'd laugh, and she'd cast an evil eye. It was an exhausting day but well worth the trip.

For Derek's eleventh birthday we planned a day at the movies and lunch at Friendly's with his friends. He began counting the days before the party, but as the day approached, meteorologists forecasted snow for the weekend. That Friday I called his friends' parents and told them we'd wait to see what happened before confirming the party. As the snow began to fall, Charlie and I sat him down and told him there was a chance the party would have to be postponed. We watched as the snow began to pile up and by the time he went to bed, almost a foot accumulated.

Early the next morning I called the parents to postpone the party and tried to reschedule it for winter break. Most of the families had prior commitments and we couldn't pick a *snow* date. Derek sulked for most of the day, but his mood changed when Jessica brought Nikki and Fayth over to celebrate.

The next day I prepared for Christmas dinner for the family even though another storm was predicted. Christmas was a wash, too. No one was able to drive up or down our hill, so the three of us spent the day without company. I made dinner for everyone two days later and Derek did get to go to the movies with a friend during winter break, but it wasn't what we had hoped for.

Sometime after New Year's I made a commitment to find a different job. Without sufficient health insurance coverage or a retirement plan, turning fifty was looking pretty bleak. I read the classifieds every Sunday, to no avail, hoping that I'd find a job with a law firm that offered the benefits I needed.

Finally, just before the end of the school year, I saw an ad in the paper looking to hire an administrative aide at the mental health department. The county offered all of the benefits I was looking for and I had the qualifications they required. The next day I gathered quite a few references and sent them off with my application and resume. Within a week or so I got a call to go in for an interview.

Just my luck, the night before my interview I got a sore throat and, when I woke up the next day, I had lost my voice. I could call to reschedule, but chances were I wouldn't get the job, so I went. When I checked in at the front desk I did my best to speak as loudly as I could, but the result was a mere whisper. The receptionist called up to administration and the director's assistant came down to great me. When I tried to explain that I had lost my voice the night before, she looked as though she would burst out laughing. There was no doubt in my mind that, as we walked toward the office, she thought I was nuts.

After being introduced to the director, I whispered "I'm so sorry, I lost my voice this morning. I didn't want to make a bad impression by canceling this interview. If you don't mind, I'll do my best to answer your questions and come back for an additional interview if you can't understand my answers."

The director laughed and turned to his assistant who nodded to him. I whispered answers to the questions as best as I could, was given a bit of dictation to take in shorthand and, surprisingly, read it back without a mistake. After what seemed like a very long and torturous time, they thanked me for coming and said they would be in touch.

About a week or so after the interview I got a call from the director and was offered the job. I accepted with the provision that I be able to take our vacation to Rhode Island in August.

Before starting the county position, we met for Derek's CSE. The Annual Review indicated that, although he was improving educationally, he had great difficulty developing new relationships. In outdoor play he'd sometimes follow groups of children, but not engage in their games. Classmates often became annoyed with him because he'd growl when he had difficulty verbally expressing himself. During class playtime he preferred to play with the computer or read. But, "He enjoyed music."

Again, social difficulties were getting in his way and, though most adults could overlook his behaviors, the kids couldn't. It was obvious he wasn't picking up social cues that other kids his age had already mastered. But, by the end of the meeting it was decided that, with a lot of modifications and positive re-enforcement, Derek would move up to fifth grade.

The first day of the new job I dropped Derek off at BOCES and drove up the hill to *Mental Health*. And, as I walked up the steps and into the building, I looked forward to my new experience.

The first week was one of adjustment. I had to learn a variety of different programs on the computer and a little about each unit. Each secretary took a turn helping with mail and working in the reception area. By the second week I began to get a little bit of work, but by the third week I was bored stiff. I spoke to my supervisor and he promised there would be plenty of work waiting for me when I returned from vacation.

Rhode Island became one of our favorite places to visit. We loved our rented house a mile from the ocean and Galilee was one of our favorite little towns. We spent most of our days at Scarborough Beach. The guys spent hours in the water jumping through the waves, boggy boarding and collecting sand in their bathing suits. I'd go in every once in a while but cherished the opportunity to lie on the beach and soak up the sun. We took an occasional walk on the beach and ran away from braking waves while picking up shells and sea glass.

Point Judith meant clam cakes, lobster, salt water taffy, and so much more. We played mini golf, went to the aquarium in Mystic, Connecticut, drove to Newport for an afternoon and took the ferry to Block Island. We had a wonderful week in the sun and neither of us wanted to leave. Unfortunately, we had to.

When I returned to work nothing much had changed. I roamed the hallways looking for work and volunteered to help wherever I could. One day a counselor from the Family and Child Unit asked if I would mind helping them make copies of flyers, stuffing envelopes, and processing information received from applications for a program called *Kids Together*—KT.

When I read the flyers and examined the application I realized that the KT Program was designed for children with ADHD symptomology. I sat there in my cubby with my mouth wide open just staring at the paper in my hands. I wondered if Derek would qualify for this group and I didn't hesitate a second to ask.

"Hi, Erika. This is Pat. I just read the Kids Together flyer and I have a question."

"Okay."

"My son has ADHD and I've been searching all over the county for a group just like this one. Is there any way to get him in the program," I asked.

She replied, "There may be one slot available. Why don't you fill out the application and I'll see what we can do."

I hung up the phone, filled out the application in record time, and ran it across the hall for Erika to review.

The next day she called and told me that they found a place for Derek in the younger group. Within the next few weeks he would start a journey that would give him the undeniable knowledge that he belonged. It was music to my ears.

SEPTEMBER ELEVENTH

It was a warm, sunny day in early September. We went through our usual morning routine, fighting for the bathroom and rushing out the door. Charlie went to his job near the Ashokan Reservoir, Derek got on the bus, and I drove to work. I greeted the security guard, stopped at the receptionist's desk, and checked to see if I knew anyone in the waiting area while I waited for the elevator. A couple of clinicians followed behind me and were in deep conversation. Apparently, they heard a news bulletin on their way in. "Did you hear the bulletin," one of them asked.

"No, what's going on?"

"They said a plane hit the World Trade Center."

When we reached the second floor, I hurriedly walked through Administration toward my cubby to find out what was happening. As soon as I put my keys on the desk, my phone rang. It was Jessica.

"Mom, did you hear the news?"

"Yeah, I heard a plane hit one of the Twin Towers."

"Do you have access to a TV?" she asked.

"I think so. Why, what's happing?"

I sensed fear in her voice as she began to describe what she was watching on TV.

"Mom, they're showing a plane flying right into one of the towers. It's not a small plane, it's a jet."

"Jess, I'll call you right back. I'm going to look for a TV."

I found one of the guards sitting in the hallway and asked where the closest television was. There was one downstairs, but I had to get permission from the director to have it turned on. As I headed back toward Administration, I passed a counselor who told me the second tower was hit.

I heard my phone ringing as I turned the corner toward my desk and grabbed it.

"Good morning. This is Pat Stroh in admin—"

"Mom, the second tower was hit."

"Jess, I'm sure this is a terrorist attack. Hold on while I find an administrator."

"Wait," she gasped. The planes were hijacked and there are others missing. They're not on their flight course."

I had no choice, I had to interrupt the director's management meeting. My immediate concern was that one of our clients would walk through the door with a report of the attack and cause panic in the waiting room.

"Jess, hold on."

I went to the conference room, knocked on the door before opening it, apologized for the interruption, and told everyone the news.

The team immediately disbursed and ran to their offices. I followed the deputy director and watched as he attempted to get onto the internet. He couldn't get in. I ran back to the phone.

"Jessica, what's happening?"

"The tower just collapsed, there's nothing left! Oh, my God. It's horrible."

"Stay with me. Don't get off the phone."

"I won't. They think the planes are heading for the White House. We're under attack."

I held my breath as I imagined the worst, then, "Oh, my God, Mom, the second tower collapsed."

Her TV lost reception and she tried to get online.

"Mom, I have to call Ed at the school. I'll call you back as soon as I can."

Mental Health was in a controlled sense of panic, afraid of what lay ahead, yet careful not to over react. There would be repercussions felt throughout the entire community and it was the department's responsibility to hold everything together.

I couldn't reach Charlie. There was no phone at the property and cell phones were not an option. I tried to call the school, but the phone was busy.

My phone rang again.

"Mom, the school is dismissing early, they have to get the kids who live past the reservoir home right away."

"Why the reservoir, I asked."

"They're afraid it might be in jeopardy because the water feeds the city."

"God, I hope Charlie knows what's going on. "Are they putting the kids on the bus?"

"I'm not sure. I'm getting Nikki now."

I tried the school again and got through. I didn't want Derek to take the bus home and the secretary promised to keep him in the school until I got there. I hung up the phone, grabbed my purse, told the director I was leaving, and ran down the stairs to the car. I listened to the radio as I drove down Route 28 and heard reports that the Pentagon was hit and another plane was still missing.

When I walked into the school, I heard excitement in the children's voices. They wore big smiles on their faces, absolutely elated that the school district decided to give them the afternoon off. I looked at Derek's teacher and whispered, "They don't know what's going on, do they?" She shook her head and replied, "They don't have a clue." When I pulled in the driveway, to my relief, Charlie was waiting for us at the door. Derek ran into his room to play a video game and Charlie and I looked at each other in disbelief.

He said that the crew was listening to the radio and thought the report was a joke. When they realized it wasn't, they packed up their trucks and headed home. Everyone leaving the reservoir area was stopped and questioned before they were allowed to proceed. Afraid that Derek would be dropped off by the bus, he drove straight home and waited.

Our first inclination was to turn on the TV and watch the news, but we had to tell Derek what was going on. There was no way to keep an attack of this magnitude from him so we sat him down and explained the events of the day. He wanted to know where the terrorists were from and asked why they hated us so much. He questioned the distance between New York City and Boiceville and wondered whether we were targets. He seemed to accept our theory that the terrorists had no desire to attack the mountains, excused himself, and went back to his game.

Charlie turned the TV on and the two of us just sat, eyes glued, watching the devastation. A little while later Derek came back into the living room, sat next to me and whispered, "Mom, I heard something outside. I think it might be terrorists."

Intellectually, I knew the terrorists weren't planning an attack in our back yard, but for a moment I was afraid.

"No, Derek. I promise, there isn't anyone in our backyard but, if you feel safer, I'll lock the doors."

An hour or so later I called our friends' house to see if they were going ahead with their sons' birthday party. All the parents agreed to go ahead with the plans in order to keep the kids' evening as normal as possible.

When we got to their house we were greeted by rambunctious kids and shell-shocked adults. The kids ran around as though nothing had happened and the parents gathered by the picnic table and spoke about war, politics, our insatiable thirst for oil, and our dwindling economy.

Somewhere between my second or third glass of wine I imagined what it would be like to send a son to war. And, for a split second I was relieved that Derek had been diagnosed with CP and ADHD. After all, the armed services didn't take kids with learning disabilities." Or so I thought.

Charlie and I were glued to the TV for weeks. The teachers in our district were very careful in their approach with the children. After completing a letter writing campaign to a New York City Fire Department to express their sadness, their subjects returned to math, social studies, and English.

LIVES RETURN TO "NORMAL"

Most of the children in Derek's class had moved up with him. Unfortunately, mold was detected in the school, making quite a few classrooms uninhabitable. The district didn't have the funding to build an addition so the kids were relegated to attend classes on the stage and the cafeteria, which also converted to a gym. The room chosen for Derek's fifth grade class was the size of a walk-in closet with a couple windows and a door. I understood that, because the kids were easily distractible, they wouldn't be able to concentrate in an open space, but the motivation for an over-crowded room made no sense. In a *normal* situation, Derek had a lot of difficulty sitting still and continued to have difficulty with personal space.

I was extremely unhappy. For most of Derek's young life I had to fight for him to succeed and he had accomplished much. I wasn't willing to sit idly by watching a good district turn bad because a few people were unwilling to pay a little more school tax to fund a healthy environment. Some of the school's board members threatened budget cuts to the Special Education Department to help fund building repair and I found a group of parents adamantly opposed to their proposition. I attended the September school board meeting and made my first speech during the segment called, "Public Be Heard." Some of my words fell on deaf ears, but I sensed that there were a few members who listened.

A little over a month into the school year, Derek's teacher called to tell me that Derek was having trouble concentrating. She said he was wiggling in his seat, becoming inappropriately angry when a student accidentally rubbed against his desk, and growled at the aide when she hovered over him. As I listened to her ramble, I couldn't help but shake my head. She taught him last year. His diagnosis hadn't changed, his IEP was the same, and he didn't miraculously become hyper focused. Besides, did she think the closet sized room would have a positive effect?

Before the conversation ended it was agreed that she would send home notes about his behavior, attempt to redirect his attention, and change his seating. I promised to work on his behaviors at home and to reward him with yummy treats if he did his best to concentrate. The rewards worked for a while, but they weren't the answer.

As Halloween approached I made Derek's costume in preparation of the big day. Even though the kids were ready for pumpkin carving night, the usual costume parade, and visions of large amounts of candy in their heads, the adults were subdued. We were still in shock over the events of 9/11. The barrage of news, the uncertainty of our security, the "War on Terror," and our nation's response in Afghanistan, was weighing heavily on our minds. But, as parents, we did our best to protect our children and maintain a sense of normalcy. By the time the holiday concert was scheduled, the rhetoric and stories of citizens stocking up with duct tape were part of our everyday conversation.

With the exception of a few squeaks and the off drumbeat, I made it through the orchestra and band performances without getting a headache. The thunderous applauds gave the chorus their cue to take to the risers. As the kids took their places, I watched to see where Derek would be standing. Then, to my amazement, I realized that he wasn't in the mix at all. They had him positioned next to the older and taller kids on the risers, but he stood all alone on the floor. If he had a solo, standing alone would great, but he didn't.

Charlie looked at me and whispered, "What's going on?"

"Take a guess. I'll be back in a few minutes."

I excused myself as I walked toward the end of the isle, went up toward the front of the room where one of the aides was standing, and asked, "What *is* going on? Who made the decision to do this to him?" She looked at me with the same, sad, sympathetic eyes I had seen so many times before and said, "I know, honey, it's horrible."

If steam really came out of my ears there would have been enough to cloud the entire room. I was fuming. I knew more than anyone how difficult it was for him to stand still and I knew he could annoy the kids, but this was not the solution.

There he was, my boy, standing alone, watching the music teacher's direction and singing the songs with an embarrassed smile on his face. He wiggled in unison as the audience watched their children.

When I got back to my seat, Charlie put his hand on my leg. We glanced at each other in despair and made sure that Derek saw us raise our hands in the air applauding for him alone. As soon as the performance was over, we swept him away from the group, left the building, and went home.

The next day I wrote to the principal and the music teacher expressing my disgust. Derek got an apology and I was promised it would never happen again. They thought they knew how hurt we were, but they had no idea.

The pain of the chorus night from hell having subsided, it was once again time to think of birthdays and holidays. My mother and I decided to take Jessica, Derek, Nikki and Fayth to see the Radio City Christmas Show.

We took the train to Grand Central, hopped in a cab and went to the theater. The kids were overwhelmed by its beauty. When we got to our seats I made sure that Derek got the aisle seat just in case he wanted a snack, got bored, or wanted to spend most of the time in the bathroom playing his Gameboy.

Fayth had difficulty seeing over the heads of the people in front of her so I put her on my lap. As soon as the Rockettes came out it was obvious Fayth was entranced. She bounced to the music as her little feet moved to the beat. Gradually she slipped off my lap and began imitating the steps of the dancers as she stood on the floor. Then, she slipped past Derek and, while maintaining her focus on the dancers, made her way to the aisle. We tried to quietly direct her back to the seats, but no luck. There she stood, with eyes focused, imitating every step. With unbalanced kicks she crept closer to the stage. Audience members turned to watch her until Jessica pulled her back into her seat. But the rhythm never stopped. She danced in the train all the way back to Poughkeepsie and that night it was decided that Fayth's Christmas present would be dance lessons.

Derek's twelfth birthday and Christmas went by quickly. He got the Game Cube he begged for and a few video games he wanted. These kept him busy through the holidays.

He was getting older and a bit more independent. Charlie and I relished the fact that we could leave him alone for a half hour or so while we ran to the store or into town. But, along with age and independence came puberty. He was still very immature for his age, but his hormones and outbursts of anger were definitely beginning to slip into his everyday behavior. He was more aware of his difficulties and was less likely to be calmed with conversation.

Kids Together was the perfect place to vent. So many of the other parents were experiencing the same frustrations and it felt good to know we weren't the only people in the world going crazy. The counselors gave us advice and common sense approaches to the kids' behaviors and our reactions. When I was young, my parents would sometimes count to ten before blowing off steam. We were taught to use the pause button before lashing out at Derek, and, in turn, he was taught how to communicate with us without losing his temper. The groups became our weekly retreat and we never missed a night.

Unfortunately, the school situation got increasingly worse. Derek's teacher started calling me weekly about his inability to concentrate. She worried that he was falling behind and I was convinced that a more appropriate classroom and a "special" educator, with an understanding of Derek's ADHD, would benefit him greatly. I developed a *voice* at board meetings, speaking on behalf of Derek and his classmates. I became active in a campaign to elect people who I thought would support the school's much needed addition and our special needs children. I got familiar with a variety of educators and felt as if I was an intricate part of the school district.

The night of the election I went to the high school and waited for the tallies to come in. The results were astounding. The funding of the addition was approved, the special education programs were safe, and the people I fought so hard for were voted in. We walked to the cafeteria and waited for the official vote. When the results were read I felt a great sense of relief and pride. That evening I felt as though I was a positive force in creating a better educational community for our son.

A month after the election the "Kids Together" program held their year-end closing. Derek received quite a few certificates for social awareness and his ability to communicate with the group. He passed fifth grade and, though he still had a lot of work to do, he was headed for sixth grade.

Charlie decided it was time for us to take a vacation in Maryland — to pack up the car and go wherever the journey led us. Even though I was a little reluctant, I agreed to Charlie's plan as long as I could reserve a campsite for a couple of days before heading home.

The trip down through Jersey went well. We made it to the Cape May Ferry in plenty of time and enjoyed the trip to Lewes, Delaware. I worried that we wouldn't be able to find a hotel in the height of the season, but after checking out a few places we decided on a motel not far from our destination. It was a small family owned place on the bay and close to the state beach.

That night we had dinner on the deck of the motel and took in the sun. The pool was small, but clean, and Derek had a grand time jumping in while Charlie and I slurped down a few glasses of wine. After he splashed half the water out of the pool, with purple lips and the blonde hair on his legs standing on end, we went upstairs to our room. Before going to bed we talked about our ideas for the following day. Derek wanted to go to a waterslide park.

We woke up to a gloomy day without a hint of sun in the forecast. Neither Charlie nor I were thrilled with the prospect of spending a lot of money for a water park in the rain, but Derek wasn't giving in. We agreed to take a ride, look around, and decide which one we'd go to if the clouds blew over.

There were plenty of amusement parks, arcades, mini-golf places, and water parks to pick from. We checked the prices and hours of operation of each and every one and did our best to direct his attention to the one that seemed to have the best rides for the least amount of money.

"Derek, that looks like a great place to go. Hopefully tomorrow will be sunnier and we'll go then," I said.

"But, Mom, I really want to go today. Can't we please go today," he begged.

"It's drizzling. I think we should wait."

"Tomorrow might be bad, too, you know."

I never liked water parks. I was a chicken and could never be coaxed to go on a slide. I liked nice heated wave pools or lazy rivers and the chance to sit in the sun, catching rays, while watching the guys run from one slide to another.

Charlie and Derek didn't care about the weather and I was outnumbered. They had a great time together while I watched after the towels and spoke to other people unwilling to play in the cold. One slide was enormous, with a slope that concerned me. But, there they were, standing on the top, waving their hands and screaming at me to watch. I thought I would lose my stomach as they took their positions and sped down the slide. At one point I was so afraid that Derek was going to go off the edge that I yelled out before covering my eyes. I think the two of them went down that thing three or four times just to watch me panic.

We went to Ocean City a couple times, played mini-golf, swam in the ocean, built sandcastles, and ate a lot of those yummy French fries with apple cider vinegar and salt. Our last day in Maryland was spent in Chincoteague, running away from enormous mosquitoes along a trail in search of wild horses, then retreating to the beach.

The campsite we chose was on the northeastern shore of Delaware. It was a brutally hot and humid day and neither of us were thrilled with the prospect of pitching the tent and unloading our gear. There was little shade on our site and Charlie was less than happy with it. Instead of a quiet area snuggled in the woods, we were right in the middle of tightly configured campsites without a hint of privacy. The three of us grumbled as we set up camp, then changed into our bathing suits, grabbed our towels, and headed for the beach.

Thankfully, not only was the water fairly warm and the sand great for castle building, but the dolphins that swam close to the shore were an absolute delight. We swam beyond the crashing waves and watched as they jumped out of the water less than a hundred yards away.

We stayed at the beach for most of the day swimming, building sand castles, and soaking up too much sun. With sand in our bathing suits, red faced and tired, we headed back to camp. Charlie made dinner while Derek talked to a cute young girl in the adjoining campsite as I set the table.

We stayed up later than usual hoping the air would cool when the sun went down, but it didn't. I tossed and turned all night long and heard Charlie and Derek do the same. First the sleeping bags got thrown off, then the sheets, and before morning the three of us were lying face up with our arms and legs outstretched, sweating like the three pigs.

Our last couple days of vacation were spent at the beach with the breeze of the ocean and an occasional walk down paths at night where World War II forts and observation decks still stood.

The drive back home was horrible. The heat wave sent throngs of people to the beaches along the Jersey shore and we sat in bumper to bumper traffic for hours. With every inch we took, Charlie moaned, Derek grunted, and I shook my head. It was 105 degrees and we were at a dead stop in traffic when our car's air-conditioner gave out. Needless to say, the Catskill Mountains were a sight for sore eyes.

A couple days after the trip, as we sat on the deck for dinner, I asked Derek what his favorite part of the trip was.

He replied, "What do you think? The waterslide park, of course."

NEGOTIATING CURVES

Funding for the school's new addition included trailers that would house the children while the internal construction took place. Derek and I waited with other parents, students, the principal, and teachers for the arrival of the temporary classrooms. We helped set up the rooms, carried books, tables and chairs, and were one of the first in the district to see the space that Derek and his friends would spend the better part of sixth grade in. It was encouraging to know that any of us could make a positive change if we stayed committed to the cause.

I was elated to see the excitement on the kids' faces as they arrived for the first day of class. They were thrilled to see a room larger than last year's with book shelves, pictures, and most of all, space. As for the parents, I could tell that they, too, were encouraged by the change. We spoke of commitment, enthusiasm and fortitude when it came to our children and looked forward to a brighter future.

Unfortunately, within weeks of the move I realized that my hopes and dreams for Derek would have to be adjusted once again. Just before pumpkin carving night I was back in the school speaking to the teacher. She continued to have serious concerns that Derek wouldn't be at grade level as he entered junior high and said she felt that he needed more attention than she was able to provide. She suggested other classes within the district and, as always, nothing fit.

Another round of testing was scheduled and several weeks were spent taking him to a psychologist in Kingston. This time he tested lower than usual and his ability to focus was, again, a determining factor.

One of our doctors at Mental Health agreed to evaluate him, give a proper diagnosis, and recommend a change in his medication. She saw Derek on several occasions and, after the report was typed, sat down with me to review her findings.

I had a lot of faith in her skills and understanding of children with a variety of diagnoses and had no doubt that she would come up with the answers we needed.

She told me that Derek was a handsomely devilish young man who worked very hard to please her. He did his best to complete the tasks needed to evaluate him, but lacked focus. We discussed his difficulties in social interaction, his repetitive patterns of behavior, physical clumsiness, and speech difficulties. And, before the meeting was over, the diagnosis of Asperger's Disorder was added to his list.

By the time we met with Derek's regular doctor and received the prescription for his new medication, the winter holidays had past and we were heading toward the home stretch in the school year. The medicine began to kick in, but not in time to change the teacher's decision to remove him from her class. There was no time to get him caught up to the other kids and junior high was on the horizon, so what better situation could there be but to place him in the class I had fought against for so many years. He certainly couldn't be placed in a *regular* class and the one that fit the bill educationally was filled with older kids who would gobble him up socially.

The adrenalin rush I experienced at the beginning of the year dwindled to a depression felt in my heart and the pit of my stomach. It felt like I failed my son, that my hard work and advocacy meant nothing. His current class work focused on general math, history, general science, and English and he was relegated to a class that taught kids how to count money, eventually availing him of the opportunity to visit a store to shop for groceries.

As we walked back into the school Derek had attended from kindergarten through second grade, it seemed as though the few good years he had at Bennett were washed away. I held his hand tightly as we walked down the hall, knocked on the door, and entered the room.

"Hi, it's so good to see you. We are so happy to meet Derek," the aide exclaimed. To my surprise, Derek seemed relieved. The anxiety of spending every day feeling like he didn't belong must have been horrible for him.

I left that day, holding back tears as I attempted to resolve this move in my mind. Derek seemed happy and, even though I knew it was a big step back educationally, we had no choice. Derek was in the "Life Skills" class.

His teacher possessed the same gentle smile and positive attitude as Mrs. Thongs and sent us one good report after the other. Derek was thrilled that the pressure was off, but I was extremely worried about his education. His class work simply repeated lessons he received years before and his friends at Bennett were slipping away. I knew he was in the wrong class, but no matter how hard I advocated for him, there was no place for him to go. Besides, not everything was discouraging. He seemed to be the class charm. The teachers and aides loved him and the children accept him with open arms.

Derek began spending time with Ed's nephew, Chris. Jessica had encouraged the two of them to get together. They attended the same school, were close in age, and were both in need of a friend. After a while, he was coming over just about every Saturday and would occasionally drag his younger brother, Raymond, along. For Derek's thirteenth birthday, the boys stayed at the house for the night and the next day we took them to the movies and dinner, reveling in the knowledge that he had friends again.

The addition at Bennett was close to completion, his old classmates and friends were about move into the renovation. I straggled into board meetings when the special education department was threatened, but my heart wasn't in it. I became less involved, not only because of my dissatisfaction with Derek's current educational situation, but I now felt inferior to the people involved in the district's activities. I was uncomfortable around adults who seemed more intelligent than me and it was difficult to watch their kids excel. I didn't have the fire in my belly anymore.

The Kids Together Program accepted our family, so I was happy to work with them. And, when my boss asked for my help organizing a conference for parents and counselors, I jumped at the chance. If there was any aspect of my job that gave me pleasure it was KT. I felt as if I was able to help parents who found themselves caught up in the mire of the mental health system. Even though I felt like a failure to Derek, I had acquired a good deal of knowledge pertaining to the special education process.

One day as I was running around at work, trying to get pamphlets and applications ready for the conference, I got a call from Jessica.

"Mom, I have something to tell you and I'm not sure how you're going to take it."

"Yeah," I replied. "What's up?"

"Well, I'm pregnant," she said.

Twice before I was concerned about her pregnancies. She was so young when she had Nikki and after her difficulties with Fayth's birth, I didn't think she'd have another child. But, I was out of lecture material.

"Congratulations, Jess."

"Thanks, Mom."

"When's the baby due," I asked.

"We have to wait for confirmation, but I think it's mid-October."

"Are you going to find out if it's a girl or a boy?

"Yup, as soon as I can arrange for a sonogram we'll find out. We're hoping it's a boy."

By the end of our conversation I think she was in shock. I didn't barrage her with my typical questions because, by this time, I had learned that her life was consumed with motherhood.

In preparation of Derek's graduation from sixth grade, I took him to the store to buy him a shirt, tie, and a pair of dress pants. He loved the shirt and tie but was less impressed with the pants, complaining that they itched too much. I didn't give in. I wanted him to look nice for the event so he was wearing them whether he liked them or not.

During the ceremony the principal was sure to acknowledge each child by handing them a special award with their diplomas. I watched Derek in the back of the group as he began to fidget. Having a last name starting with "S" was difficult for him to sit through and I watched as one of the teachers motioned for him to settle down. By the time his name was called, he jumped up, walked to the center of the stage, gave us a big "Derek" smile, and accepted his diploma and award. As he turned, I looked at my gorgeous graduate, his beautiful blonde hair, the neatly pressed shirt and tie, his brand new shoes, and the pants which appeared to be shredded from the knee up. I turned to Charlie and said, "Whoops, I guess I should have listened to him."

To celebrate the momentous event we planned a camping trip to North-South Lake and invited Chris and Raymond to come along. Not long after we arrived, Derek showed the guys he knew a little something about camping. He helped Charlie put up the tent and dig the proverbial trench, then took the boys on a walk in search of wood. After dinner Charlie made a roaring fire and we toasted marshmallows while the guys shared spooky stories.

The next day, after Charlie left for a bike ride, we headed toward the beach. While the kids walked ahead of me I couldn't help but notice that Chris was tormenting Raymond—teasing and prodding him along the way. I suppose I should have realized that brothers have a tendency to do that but, I couldn't take it. Raymond was obviously upset so, to diffuse the situation, I told them if they spent their energy making it to the lake without being mean to one another, I'd rent a canoe.

As soon as we planted our feet in the sand, the boys threw their towels down and headed for the boats. "Whoa," I yelled. "Come with me. I have to pay for it first. Besides, you need life jackets."

After explaining why we needed to wear the jackets, I showed them how to get in the boat and where to sit. After all, I'd been canoeing before and who better to teach them but me. After I was sure they got the gist of it, I placed my towel, suntan lotion, and camera in the boat. I pushed it out far enough in the water to keep it stable, put one foot in the middle, reached down to hold onto the seat, and began to enter. As soon as I lifted my other leg, I felt the canoe move away from me and, as I lost my balance, it tipped over.

There I was, laying half in the canoe, half in the lake, my towel in the water with the suntan lotion and camera floating away. I screamed "Get the camera." Chris grabbed it as I pulled myself out of the boat, looking around to see if anyone else witnessed my stupidity. If I avoided the embarrassment of having other beachgoers seeing what I had done, the kids grabbed their attention. The three of them were laughing so hard they could hardly contain themselves. After they calmed down and I drained the camera of water, Chris took charge.

With the exception of Raymond getting a little red from the sun, the rest of the afternoon went well. The kids enjoyed the lake and, as usual, it took a lot of coaxing before Derek agreed to get out of the water.

The rest of our mini-vacation was spent swimming, hiking, sitting in front of a campfire and telling stories. Although we got along pretty well, there were conflicts. Derek spent some time sulking in the tent,

Chris and Raymond chastised each other, and Charlie and I worked trying to keep it all together. As a whole, the experience went well and I realized two things: Chris was going to be replaced by Raymond as Derek's best friend and, never put your camera in a canoe if you don't know what you're doing.

We decided that summer school at BOCES wasn't doing enough for Derek, socially. So, we registered him for camp in town with the rest of the kids from school. He got the bus at the end of our road, hung out with a few kids he knew from previous years, and spent most of his days swimming. Raymond started coming over more often than Chris and stayed overnight on Saturdays every once and a while.

BALANCE

A week or so before school started we attended junior high orientation. After the principal spoke to the crowd of anxious parents and students, we were disbursed to different classrooms. There we met the teacher designated to watch Derek's progress and help him negotiate through seventh grade. While we listened to her speak, it was evident that she had read his records and that she, too, was *unimpressed* with his most recent move. She spoke of Derek's learning disabilities as though they were obstacles he might be able to overcome and I was given hope once again. I heard compassion in her voice, while steadfast in her commitment to his education. She would not let Derek slide through and that spoke volumes.

The first couple of weeks went well. He seemed to negotiate through the hallways and met friends from Bennett during lunch and gym. I appreciated the reprieve from anxiety and looked forward to receiving news of goals achieved.

In the meantime, Jessica and Ed were preparing for the birth of their baby boy. Jessica planned to have a cesarean section and needed to have tests run in Albany in order to schedule the delivery. She was experiencing all kinds of medical difficulties and her doctor wanted to be sure the baby was healthy enough to be delivered prematurely. The tests were run and the doctors assured them that the baby was healthy and strong enough should the delivery be earlier than expected. Of course, we hoped that she'd be able to hang on as long as possible, but neither she nor the baby could wait. Dakota was born on September 24, 2003.

Ed called me at work to tell me that Jessica was fine, but the baby wasn't doing well. Dakota was having difficulty breathing and had to be transferred to a Neonatal Intensive Care Unit.

As soon as I heard the news I shut down my computer, told the boss I was leaving, and set my sights on Northern Dutchess Hospital. On the way I thought of Derek, his diagnoses, and everything he had gone through since birth. No matter how many times the doctors denied it, I knew that his difficulties were the result of his delivery and I worried that Dakota was in jeopardy.

Ed was waiting for me in the hallway of the birthing center and brought me to Jessica's room. At first glance she looked remarkably calm and said, "Mom, they cleared him for delivery but they were wrong. He can't breathe on his own."

I stood next to her bedside and did my best to keep her calm, but when I asked her if she was going with Dakota, the floodgates opened and she cried, "No, I have to stay here until I'm cleared for discharge. I want to be with my baby!"

Ed followed the ambulance and I stayed with Jessica until she was able to be alone. She needed to rest and heal quickly to be with her little boy, so I didn't linger.

With fingers crossed, she was released within twenty-four hours and went directly to the hospital where she stayed until Ed came in for the night shift. I spent time traveling back and forth to the hospital during the week and brought Charlie and Derek to see the little guy over the weekend. It was obvious by the look on their faces that they were concerned. Derek blew a kiss to his nephew, then turned to Jessica, rubbed her back, and gave her a kiss. It was a gentle moment and one I will never forget. Thankfully, after an eight day stay, Dakota was given a clean bill of health and released from the hospital.

Derek continued to do well in school. His lead teacher pushed him just a little harder and gave him more challenging work than the others. Each time we spoke, she expressed her belief that he should be removed from life skills and placed in a higher skilled class. Before the end of the second semester, we scheduled a meeting with the special education department. At that point, I was tired of going at it alone so I contacted the Resource Center for Accessible Living. They had staff that reviewed students' records and who represented children at district meetings. We needed the support of someone who could think objectively and out of the box.

Susan knew a lot about the various school districts in our area. She had been on the job for quite some time and was not afraid of sticking up for Derek's rights. During the meeting we sat at a table of educators and social workers. She listened to their evaluations and their understanding of his past and when they were finished she asked them questions about his behavior and his social interaction. Then she asked, "Doesn't this sound like a developmental disorder to anyone at the table?" With erythematic nodding in the affirmative, it appeared as though they were instantly enlightened by this new train of thought. And, before the meeting was concluded, Derek was cleared for yet another round of testing by a doctor at the Annex in Kingston.

A week or so after the testing was complete, Derek and I to went back to visit with the doctor. After checking in with the receptionist, Derek paced up and down the hallway while I pretended to glance through the facility's pamphlet. We were both tired of the process but anxiously awaited a diagnosis that made sense.

As soon as the doctor poked her head out of the door and motioned to us, we followed her into the office. We listened to her as she described the findings in her report and, as usual, the results were all over the place. His educational level ranged from three years below grade average to three or four years above average. We discussed his inability to pick up social cues and difficulty maintaining friendships.

Derek listened as our conversation continued and responded to questions with a nod of his head or muted grumbles. He had heard it all before and had become frustrated with the entire process. He hated his class, became increasingly annoyed with his classmates, and wanted nothing to do with the aides. He was a thirteen year-old who yearned for acceptance outside the confines of our home and waited for something positive.

About an hour into the meeting the doctor began to read her recommendations.

Derek did not belong in the life skills class. She wanted him in an integrated program receiving the benefit of classes with "regular" kids and she insisted that he become involved with a sport that might encourage friendships.

Her diagnosis was something I had never heard of before; not ADHD, ADD, or Asperger's. It was Pervasive Development Disorder— PDD. As I listened to the definitions of the disorder, it made sense. Derek sat there with an inquisitive look on his face, not sure what to make of this new revelation.

After we spoke about alternatives for social interaction and a change in his curriculum, I thanked her for meeting with us, shook her hand, and left with the recommendation in hand.

As we walked to the car Derek asked, "Mom, can I say … what the hell?"

"Yup, you can." I replied.

"What was she talking about? What do I have now?"

I thought for a minute and said, "Derek, as far as I'm concerned you suffer from what we will call the *ABCDEFG* disorder from now on."

"What?"

"Let's face it kiddo. It doesn't matter what it is. CP, ADHD, ADD, or PD, you're a good person. We both know that you're smarter than everyone thinks and this doctor says you're moving on."

He rubbed my shoulder, I patted his knee, then leaned over to plant a kiss on his forehead.

"I love you, Mom. Thank god, I'm getting out of that stupid class."

As I drove home we sang to the radio with our windows wide open, letting the whole world know that we were cool.

With the switch in school complete, I was hell bent to find some sort of sport. Unfortunately, none of the coaches had the time or the inclination to work with a kid with social issues and lack of athletic balance. I racked my brain thinking of anything Derek could do to gain self-respect, something to boost his ego, get him exercise, and a chance to be with kids his age. He didn't want to learn how to golf, didn't want to join a swimming club, and had no ideas of his own.

One Saturday afternoon, after taking him into Kingston to see some silly teenage movie, we passed a busy ski shop in preparation for the winter season and my mind went into overdrive.

"I've got it! Derek, I have a great idea."

"Now what," he asked.

"If I found someone to give you ski lessons would you be willing to try it? Skiing isn't a contact sport and if you really like it you could join the school's ski team. What do you think?"

To my amazement he replied without hesitation, "Okay."

First thing Monday morning I set my plan in motion. An old friend from community theater was a special educator at the Junior High who also gave ski lessons at Belleayre and I knew if anyone could teach Derek, it would be Bill. He had known Derek since he was born and understood the barriers he had, not only educationally, but physically. So, when I spoke to him on the phone, he suggested I call Belleayre to schedule private lessons as soon as ski season started.

Not long after Derek's 14th birthday and the holidays were over, we headed up the mountain for his first lesson. On the way there I gave him my *I'm so proud of you for trying something new* speech and did everything I could to encourage positive thinking as we walked through the lodge. It wasn't until we were in the ski shop that I remembered how cumbersome the equipment was.

As we walked up the steps toward ski school Derek had difficulty holding the skis and poles together. They hit the bottom of the step and began to separate while the poles tangled around his wrists. I could see his blood pressure rise as we reached the second floor and, by the time we got his boots on, his face was as red as his ski jacket. After a torturous half hour of preparation he was ready for the elements. I carried his skis and he clumped his way up the hill to the lesson area where Bill was waiting. We spoke for a few minutes and, after I was assured Derek would be fine, I wished them luck, turned around and went into the lodge to hide. Every fifteen minutes or so I walked outside to see if they were coming down the mountain, but there was no sign of them. By the time an hour had past I began to have second thoughts. What if he fell and got hurt, or worse. What if he fell and gave up? Then, finally, I saw a glimpse of Bill skiing backwards with Derek holding on to his poles. He had miraculously taken Derek inch by inch down the beginner's slope. Derek was exhausted, Bill was cautiously optimistic, and I was elated.

"Derek, you did it! I'm so proud of you. Do you want to come back next Sunday," I asked.

After mumbling a couple of words under his breath he sighed, "Okay."

The next weekend he made it down the mountain twice. It was labor intensive and he was having difficulty, but his balance was improving. The following weekend he made it without Bill holding on every second with the help of a line guide but it was exhausting. His face was red, sweat poured off his forehead, and he looked like he had gone through a battle. So, when Bill asked him if he wanted to go one more time Derek turned to me and said, "Mom, I did it twice, isn't that enough?"

I thought for a second and said, "No, you have more time; I want you to go up again."

He muttered some expletive, shook his head, looked it Bill and said, "Okay, if I have to."

It took two more individual lessons before Bill set him free, but when he did Derek was a skier. The following weekend we went together. It felt good to be back on the mountain and, with the exception buckling up boots, we had a great time.

One afternoon as we made our way down the mountain Derek skied next to me and said, "Mom, wait a minute. I have something to tell you."

"What, hon?"

"I'm skiing so good, I think I'm a natural."

"Yeah Derek, you're a natural all right." That season we skied just about every weekend until the snow began to melt. We were getting ready for a trip; we were going to fly to Puerto Rico and take a cruise to the Caribbean. Skiing would have to wait until next year.

VACATION, ANYONE?

I have to admit that, at times, I feel the necessity to fit in with the "Jones'." Most of my friends were vacationing in great places, cruising and having a great adult life. We had Derek pretty late in life and, while our counterparts were enjoying their 50s, we were raising a teenager. Don't get me wrong. I didn't feel as if my life was boring. But, I wanted to cruise.

Just before the Christmas holidays, I started talking to the guys about the possibility of an island hopping vacation. Charlie wasn't particularly thrilled with the idea, but Derek was game. He loved to vacation by the water and the prospect of being able to move about the ship freely was a bonus.

So, I did everything I could to convince Charlie a cruise would be a great idea. I copied itineraries from the computer, got booklets from travel agents, spoke to my mother, Dotty, and a few others who had been to the Caribbean before. We watched videos from Carnival and other cruise lines and, finally, he caved. We booked our vacation during spring break.

This Christmas would be a celebration of our upcoming trip. I bought the guys sunglasses, water resistant watches, bathing suits, flowered shirts, swimming goggles, and sun tan lotion. I wrapped the presents and put them into two new suitcases. On Christmas Eve I placed the suitcases under the tree and hung our cruise tickets in plain sight. I was obviously obsessed and the guys were kind enough to play along.

The day before our flight we drove to a hotel near Newark airport to stay for the night. By that time, the three of us were pretty excited about the adventure and none of us could sleep. Finally, at around 5:00 a.m., we got up, packed our bags, and went down for breakfast before the shuttle picked us up. Our departure at the airport was uneventful and the flight to Puerto Rico went smoothly. Each seat on the plane had a screen that displayed a navigational system that tracked where we were and what our estimated time of arrival would be. Derek listened to music, played games, and never once looked toward the heavens.

As soon as we landed we were directed to a shuttle bus that took us to the ship. When we arrived, we were led to an area where cruise line representatives checked everyone in. A woman called out, "Is the Stroh family here?" We raised our hands, she walked over to us, pointed to our luggage, and removed the tags indicating our cabin number. For a fleeting second I questioned our reservations and wondered if I had done something wrong. She saw the panic on my face and laughed, "Don't worry, we have a great surprise. You are getting upgraded to a suite on the veranda deck."

Never having been on a cruise before we had no idea what to expect. Even though the Jubilee was one of the smallest in the fleet, we were overwhelmed by its size and astounded by the bustling crew as we made our way to our suite. When Charlie opened the cabin door our jaws dropped. We had a wet bar, a king sized bed, a queen sized couch that opened up to a bed, a whirlpool bath, and a huge deck. We jumped on the bed and looked around, amazed by our good fortune, then stepped out onto the deck and looked down at the blue water of the Caribbean for the first time.

We gazed for a while and, just before the ship was scheduled to leave port, we heard an announcement from the captain directing us to the main deck for an emergency drill. The heat of the tropics descended upon us while we watched the crew disseminate instructions should the ship take on water. Within minutes Derek began fidgeting and groaning in dissatisfaction. He had two things on his mind: the water slide and unlimited ice cream.

When the drill ended we hurried back to the cabin to deposit our life jackets. We watched the ship leave port, changed into our bathing suits and went down to the main deck. Warm tropical water filled the pool and, as soon as the deck hands were finished with their work and the depth of the water was safe, Derek jumped in. Charlie and I watched him as we sat at the bar ordering our first daily special tropical drink.

We stayed around the pool all afternoon and begrudgingly left to dress for dinner. The guys were less than happy with the dress code in the dining room, but when they saw lobster on the menu, their eyes lit up.

That night Derek went to the teen club while we tried our luck in the casino. Charlie and I ended up with a good amount of coinage and we were convinced we would win enough money during the cruise to pay our bar bill.

As far as I'm concerned the best time of a cruise is early morning as the ship prepares for entry into a new port. With a cup of coffee in hand, on our private deck, I watched as we slowly approached St. Thomas. After breakfast we packed our bags and got in line to leave the ship, passed through security, and found a bus to take us to Meagan's Bay. It was our first time experiencing a hair raising trip along the narrow, winding roads of the island, but Meagan's Bay was worth it. The view was spectacular, the water was crystal clear, and the beach sand felt like powder on my feet. We swam for quite a while before Charlie and I decided to catch some sun, but Derek continued his quest to swim with the most colorful fish he had ever seen. Every minute or so he yelled, "Mom, Dad, come here. Look at this fish."

I replied, "Derek, I saw the fish. I want to lay in the sun for a while."

"Come on, Mom. Please?"

How could I resist? I went back in the water and we swam together, looking at fish every color of the rainbow. It was a magical moment, and I was glad he was enjoying the experience, but I wanted to spend some time with Charlie on the beach.

As soon as I hit the sand he yelled, "Dad, you have to come in and see this."

I never did get the chance to lay in the sun. The three of us spent the rest of the time swimming and didn't get out of the water until a few minutes before it was time to head back to the ship. As we left Meagan's Bay, I made a promise to return.

That night, as we sat down for dinner, the ship started on its course toward Antigua. We pulled into port early that morning and prepared for our second bus trip to spend a carefree morning on a secluded white sand beach. Antigua is a stunning island with its range of mountains in the distance and painted houses of vibrant yellows, aquas and pinks. With crystal clear water, half a mile of soft white sand bordered by coconut palms and sea grape trees, the beach was beautiful. We thoroughly enjoyed our time there, swimming, feeling the marine breeze, and witnessing the incredible view.

When our time in Antigua was over, the three of us had more than enough sun, but neither of us were willing to stay in the cabin all day. So, we lathered ourselves up with as much suntan lotion as our skin could absorb and went back to the pool in the afternoon. The next island was St. Lucia. Charlie looked forward to this stop. He booked a bicycle tour around the island and to a waterfall in the forest.

After breakfast, while he was traversing the island on a rented bicycle, Derek and I learned that our tour to the beach was cancelled. So, rather than stay on board, I talked Derek into a tour of the island in a taxi cab. St. Lucia is a beautiful island, with colorful, tropical plants, luscious banana trees, and magnificent views. Our cab driver, Maxwell, told us much about the history of the island and the agreements between his government and the Chevron/Hess Oil Companies. Just before we headed toward the port, he pointed to children wearing beautiful pressed uniforms as they got off their school bus. Then, a little farther down the road he showed us the metal shacks they lived in. It was hard for me to imagine how they lived without running water, plumbing or electricity, and tried my best not to utter anything inappropriate, but Derek, in his infinite wisdom, gasped, "Holy shit!" Maxwell laughed and said, "Yes, young man. Hard to imagine, right?" As we said goodbye to our friend and walked toward the ship, I stopped Derek and asked him to look back on our very humbling experience.

Dominica seemed to be as financially strapped as St. Lucia, if not worse. The streets were lined with people trying to sell us a variety of scarves, jewelry and trinkets, and within minutes we were approached by at least ten or more taxi cab drivers willing to take us to paradise. By the time we made it down one block, Charlie decided to take Franklin up on his offer. He was a good natured cabbie who was anxious to take us to his favorite beach. It was beautiful and, again, we thoroughly enjoyed swimming in crystal clear water and strolling along the black sand beach. When it was time to head back to port he drove us through town and told us about the island's history. He showed us the street he lived on and took us into the heart of town. There, Derek was able to hop out of the cab, talk briefly to a woman at an open market, and get his first taste of papaya.

Our last stop was the Dominican Republic. There was news of political unrest and we were advised not to go into town, so we stayed on board. Several people didn't heed the warning and ran into trouble that night on their way back to the ship.

The next morning we left the port and started the trip back to Puerto Rico. By that time, Charlie was tired of spending money and cruising, but Derek and I would have been happy to stow away on board.

After departing the ship in Puerto Rico we got the shuttle back to the airport and flew back to Newark, where we picked up our car. After all the fun in the sun, the adventure of being in the Caribbean, and sipping the drinks of the day, we were heading home.

Within a day or so we transitioned back to reality. Charlie and I were back at work and Derek was back in school. As usual, between spring break and the end of May, I got a call from his lead teacher to discuss plans for the following year. Derek had reached many goals and with the help of his lead teacher and modifications, was prepared to graduate seventh grade. It was wonderful to know that hard work and advocacy was paying off. Derek was finally on the right path and I felt that it was time for me to advocate for myself.

Though I loved working with the Family and Child Unit, I was becoming discouraged with my job. I read classified ads, searched on line, and did my best to network throughout the legal community. Finally, in the Sunday morning paper I saw a help wanted ad for a legal assistant that seemed to fit. I called first thing Monday morning and got an interview at the employment agency and then with the senior partner and office manager. After the last interview I was offered the position. The benefits weren't as good as the county's and the drive would be a hassle, but the salary was great, and I needed to get back to the insanity of law.

As always, the first week on any new job can be overwhelming, but from conversations I had with others in the legal community, I could expect to be completely drained at the end of each day. Apparently, my new boss was a perfectionist who had little patience for his peers, let alone staff. Thankfully, his assistant of 20 years agreed to stay until I became acclimated with the office and the boss's quirks.

Because the firm discouraged personal calls, I explained the need for Derek to check in with me every afternoon. The boss asked that I limit my time spent on the phone and, even though I knew it would be difficult, I promised to comply. The staff at Mental Health knew Derek and his difficulty cutting to the chase, so they ignored our afternoon calls. However, this was no longer the case.

The first day or so he did pretty well. I'd remind him that we couldn't talk too long and he abided by the new rules. But, by the end of the week the conversation began to drag and the boss began to hover.

After the first few minutes, I'd say,

"Derek, I can't talk now. I have to hang up."

"But Mom, I have to ask you a question."

"What," I'd curtly reply.

"Can you stop at the mall and buy that game I told you about?"

"Not today. Derek, we'll have to talk about this later."

"Please, mom," he begged.

"I'll see."

"Great. That means no."

"Derek, I have to go. I'll see you in a little while."

"Fine."

As soon as we hung up the boss would yell, "Mrs. Stroh, have you finished that letter I dictated?" or "Mrs. Stroh, can you get me a file?"

It was pretty evident that there would be little tolerance pertaining to personal needs, so when Derek woke up with an intense headache after the second week on the job, I knew I couldn't call in sick. Thankfully, Charlie agreed to stay home, keep an eye on him, and work on the new addition he was building.

I called the guys at home during lunch hour and found out that Derek's headache was worse. Charlie thought it might be a migraine because he complained about the light, seemed to be off balance, and vomited a couple of times before falling to sleep. I rushed home after work, spoke to Charlie for a few minutes before he took off for a bike ride, and checked in on Derek.

As I approached the bed he looked up at me and moaned, "Would you rub my head?" I must have been with him for an hour when I heard a car pull into the driveway. To my surprise, Charlie's old boss Hank was standing at the door. At first I thought he might want to talk to Charlie about working with him again, but within seconds I knew that wasn't his intention.

"Pat, Charlie was hit by car."

"Where is he? Is he okay?"

"They're taking him to Benedictine Hospital. I saw the whole thing. He got hit pretty hard, but, he's alive."

"Oh my god!"

I panicked. What was I going to do? I had Derek in bed with a migraine. I couldn't leave him alone, but I had to get to Charlie. I called Trudy to see if she could sit with Derek, but it would take time for her to get to the house. My mom didn't answer her phone. Finally, I got a hold of Jessica and Hank agreed to stay at the house until she got there.

On the way into Kingston I contemplated all types of scenarios. What if he broke his back, had head injuries, or lost a limb? I prayed, "God, please don't let him die."

What would I do without him? I started to cry. Then I screamed, "No, Charlie, you are not going to die. You will be fine." By the time I reached the hospital, my brain was numb.

I rushed through the parking lot at a steady pace, head held up, looking straight forward, as if I were walking through a tunnel. The woman at the reception desk called into the emergency room and I was quickly escorted to his side. While the emergency room doctors worked on him, he tried to explain that the board he was strapped to caused him agonizing pain. He told them that his bones were broken and that he had to be taken off the board.

I paced from his bedside to the hallway waiting for someone to take him for x-rays while he reeled with pain. Each time I walked into the hall I glared at the doctors until they made eye contact with me. Finally, they lifted him off the board and took him to radiology.

While I waited for him to get back from the x-rays, I called Jessica at the house. She said that Derek was doing all right but she was concerned. I asked her to stay with him until I got home. I would deal with Derek's migraine in the morning. In the meantime, I needed to be with Charlie.

I went back to the ER and waited until he was brought back from radiology. One of the residents spoke with us briefly and mentioned that they might tape him up before releasing him. Charlie whispered something under his breath, looked at me and said, "This guy is crazy, I'm not going home. I have broken bones and I can't breathe. I think I have a punctured lung." Then he turned to the doctor and told him, in no uncertain terms, "I need a specialist to review the x-rays again." He knew exactly what his injuries were and the orthopedist confirmed that he had several broken ribs, a broken clavicle and shoulder blade, and a collapsed lung.

After hours of waiting in the emergency room he was finally admitted and brought to his room. I stayed with him until he was settled, kissed him goodnight, and left for home.

It must have been about 3:00 in the morning when I walked in the door. Jessica and I spoke for a few minutes, then Derek called me to his room. He was sitting in bed waiting to hear what happened and as soon as I told him his dad would be okay, he went back under the covers and fell fast asleep.

The next morning I sent Derek to school and went to the hospital. Charlie looked pretty banged up the night before, but by morning the bruising began to show, he had a tube in his chest, and the lacerations on his shoulders and arms looked horrible. There was hardly a place on his body that could be touched without pain and the medication he was given simply didn't work. Blood was still in his hair, on his face, and beard; and the dirt and gravel from the road was still on his arms and hands. I washed him as well as I could without moving him or touching any of the wounds and sat with him until the orthopedic surgeon examined him.

It was hard to leave his side, but I convinced myself that he might get some sleep if I went to the office. I tried to get some work done, but it was extremely difficult to focus. By midafternoon I decided to leave work early and went back to be with him for a while before going home.

The next day I arranged to meet Jessica and Derek at the hospital after work. They had been visiting with Charlie for a while before I got there and, when I walked into the room, I couldn't help but feel a bit of tension in the air. Derek's reaction to his dad's injuries were perplexing. He seemed abrupt and less than sympathetic. He seemed angry with Charlie and I was totally bewildered. On the way home I tried to get some answers. Our discussion went round and round. Derek tried to convey his thoughts as I tried to make sense of them.

Finally, as we pulled in the driveway, I realized he was upset because he thought Charlie was somehow to blame. When we walked into the house, I grabbed a piece of paper and pencil and drew the accident scene for Derek to look at. I explained that he was riding his bike down the road when he saw a car in the distance stop to let him pass before making a left turn and, as soon as he approached the car, the driver crossed the road right in front of him. He crashed into the car and flew over it, landing in the road, while witnesses watched in horror. When I reiterated that his father did nothing wrong he said calmly, "Oh, that's a relief."

Later that night we sat on the couch watching TV. Derek stretched out, put his head in my lap, and I began rubbing his head. I began to cry and he reached up, planted a soft kiss on my cheek and said, "Everything will be all right Mom. I'm sorry I got mad at Dad." He put his head back on my lap and grunted, "Rub my head."

Charlie was home within three days, though he wasn't physically ready. It was horrible to watch him in agony and it was impossible to comfort him. He went through hell for weeks—not able to sleep, to lie in bed, or sit without discomfort. It took a while before he was cleared for physical therapy, but when he was, he attacked it with fury. No one was going to prevent him from getting on a bicycle again.

He was home every afternoon when Derek got home from camp, so the phone calls at work slowed down a bit. After a while I enjoyed the freedom from worry every afternoon, but Derek felt constrained. He was used to getting off the bus and taking full advantage of the food in the cabinets and the opportunity to play video games until his fingers numbed. He couldn't wait for Charlie to go back to work.

DIVERSITY

As summer came to an end, Derek got his eighth grade schedule. He wasn't enthralled with algebra, science, English or history but, when he saw that chorus and cooking class were part of the first semester, his eyes lit up.

He got off to a good start in math and science, had at bit of trouble in history and English, but excelled at making pancakes. No aides were needed in cooking class, he was free to be himself, and was more than happy to complete his homework. It was proving to be a positive year and we saw a vast improvement in his self-image.

Raymond took the bus home with him just about every Friday after school and stayed most weekends. It was beginning to feel as if he was part of the family. The boys played video and computer games non-stop and, every once and a while, they'd bless us with their company on their way to raid the kitchen cabinets. We went through more snacks and soda than we ever had in our life but, it was worth every penny. Derek's life began to revolve around his time spent with Raymond.

He was the brother Derek always wanted and, though they got along really well, there were times that they acted like siblings. Derek was an early riser and Raymond had to be pried out of bed. Derek was the "only child" in our household and Raymond had a brother and two sisters. Derek was spoiled and Raymond couldn't understand why he got away with so much.

Saturdays were typically spent driving to Kingston to drop them off at the movies while I went grocery shopping. On the way in, Derek and I would sing the same songs over and over again, while Raymond slept in the back seat with his head leaning against the window. As usual, Derek would have his mind set on a new game he couldn't live without and tormented me in between songs.

"Mom, I really want the new Sonic game."

'How much is it," I asked.

"Only thirty dollars."

"Don't you have enough games?"

"Come on Mom, please? I'll pay you back."

The last thing I wanted to do was pay for another game, but before we reached Kingston I gave in with the promise that he would do chores around the house. He lived up to his promise that week: cleared the dinner table, emptied the dishwasher, and did his wash, so as far as he was concerned his debt was paid.

As Derek's fifteenth birthday approached, I asked if there was something special he wanted to do that day. Of course, he wanted Raymond to stay over the night before and for me to take them to Kingston in the afternoon.

Knowing recent patterns, I prepared myself for the inevitable and, when Raymond's mother called the night before to tell us that he was too sick to come over, I wasn't surprised. Derek was devastated. He didn't believe the "sick" story for a second and I immediately went into damage control.

We had just bought him a pair of used boots, a new ski jacket, helmet and other accessories for his birthday. Obviously, spending the day with me on the slopes would not be as much fun as running through the mall and going to the movies with Raymond, but it would have to be better than nothing.

It took a lot of convincing on my part but, he finally agreed.

Before leaving that morning he stopped me in the kitchen, gave me a bear hug, and a kiss on the forehead. We looked in each other's eyes and he whispered, "Thank you."

After loading up the car we said goodbye to Charlie and headed up the mountain. The ski slopes got a fresh pack of new snow the night before and the conditions would be great.

One of worst parts of skiing was getting the equipment to the lodge and then finding a place at a table to unload everything. There were no cubbies at the lower lodge so everyone left their shoes, ski bags, and ice chests all over the place.

The lodge was packed with skiers up for Christmas vacation and the lodge was a mess. Derek and I both tripped a couple times while trying to find an empty space and the frustration on our faces began to show. Finally, we found a spot that we both agreed on and got ready for the challenge of the day.

The second worst part of skiing was getting our boots snapped up. Within minutes, Derek was sweating and cursing under his breath. His face was as red as his new ski gear and I began to lose my patience with him. Sure, the boots were different than the rentals, but how bad could they be. I counted to ten, got down on my knees, placed his foot firmly on the floor, and attempted to secure them. I had a horribly difficult time getting the straps to stay closed and experienced one of my most intense hot flashes in the process, but after the two of us calmed down and the boots secured, we were ready to go.

As soon as we walked out of the lodge he complained about the boots.

"Mom, these things hurt my ankles."

I told him to deal with it until he got acclimated to the new style, but as we traveled up the mountain he complained about them again. We didn't make it down a quarter of the mountain when he stopped, stamped his poles into the snow, and slammed his skis in total anger.

"Mom, these boots hurt. I can't ski in them. I hate these boots."

"Damn it Derek, I'm doing my best to make you feel better because Raymond didn't show. I'm trying to have a good time with you. Can't I do anything to make you happy?"

"I'm telling you, these boots hurt."

"Great. When we get down the damn mountain, I'll try on your boots."

It seemed like eternity but we finally made it to the lodge. He stomped to the table and made a scene in front of everyone. I did all I could to stay composed. And, after calming him down and demanding his patience, we switched boots. We wore the same size and I was determined to show him that he was being foolish.

But before we reached the chairlift I could feel the stiffness in the upper part of the boot and had difficulty bending my legs. While we traveled up the mountain their weight and inflexibility hurt my ankles. I found myself lifting my feet every other minute to alleviate pain, and before we reached the top I put my arm around him and said, "Oh my god, Derek you were so right. These boots suck."

He replied with a huff, "I told you."

He skied down the slope with ease and I stopped every few minutes to alleviate the pain.

At the end of a short day of skiing my legs were killing me. We stopped at a friend's ski shop and learned that the boots were made for racing and definitely not made for novices like us. As you can imagine, I begged for Derek's forgiveness all the way home. It was not one of my best parenting moments.

Raymond ended up staying half of winter recess with us and the guys had a good time, but I realized this situation couldn't go on forever. It was time for Derek to diversify and I was going to make sure it happened.

Nikki was more than old enough to ski, so we rented her a ski package for the season. She learned quickly and before long the three of us were skiing together every Sunday, making great progress and having a lot of fun on the slopes. It was fantastic to watch Derek meander down the mountain ahead of me and it was hysterical to look back at Nikki with her legs outstretched, arms flailing, and screeching, "Grandma, wait for me."

Invariably, Derek would step on the back of someone else's skis while we waited to get on the lift. I'd tell him to back up, he'd get upset with me, give me a dirty look, and stomp up to the *staging* area with Nikki at his side. They'd get on the chair lift together and I would follow them with a *single* I was paired with on the lift line. Often, in between conversations, I looked up and watched the kids up ahead and heard Nikki screeching, "Derek, stop tickling me."

We always met at the top of the mountain to decide which trail to ski down. There were days that we got in ten to fifteen runs, repeating the same scenario each time.

This winter was a treat. Derek's skiing ability was awe inspiring, Nikki was growing up, and we were all outside in the cold, exercising and developing a closeness never to be forgotten. Unfortunately, the weather wasn't cooperating and the snow melted at a rapid speed. We packed the skis away for the season in late February.

By that time Derek was tired of the repetition and was thrilled that we no longer had to send Raymond home Saturday afternoons. By spring we were back to the old schedule and the guys were together entire weekends at a time. He still got angry when Raymond didn't show, but as time went on I did less to appease him. Raymond wouldn't be around forever and I wanted him to diversify his circle of friends

The Kids Together Program offered a sanctuary for Derek to speak his mind and develop relationships, but most of the kids lived in the Kingston area. They would see each other at the mall from time to time and I'd try to hook up with their parents, but it was difficult living so far away.

I asked him to get the names and phone numbers of friends from school, but he'd either forget or had no interest in asking them.

Then one day he got a call from Jesse. He was about the same age as Derek and lived ten minutes away. Apparently, he knew Raymond and the three of them were pals in school. Each of them had acquired gaming skills and an affinity for the computer so, when they wanted to spend time together, I was more than happy to accommodate.

Jesse was a bit higher on the learning curve, but he seemed to fit in with the dynamic duo. His mom was very active in the Special Education PTA and we bonded quickly. It was a breath of fresh air to be able to have a conversation with a mom who was as obsessed about her son's education as I was and, Derek had a new friend.

HEARTSICK

Not long after our last run down the mountain, I got a call from Irene. There was undeniable angst in the tone of her voice and I knew something was wrong. Danny had been sick with the flu for a while and wasn't recovering. Ordinarily a lingering flu wouldn't be too worrisome, but in his case it raised questions no one wanted to ask. Dan had been in remission for a little over fifteen years but there was always the fear that cancer might return in one form or another.

Irene's voice began to quiver as she told me that Dan was diagnosed with leukemia and that the treatments he was given to save his life years prior were a direct cause of the cancer he had now. It was a horrible diagnosis for Danny and devastating news for my sister, Matthew, Michelle, and the entire family.

Unlike the bone marrow treatment he had fifteen years before, they could no longer harvest his marrow. He needed a donor and had to hold on for as long as it took for one to be found.

Charlie, Derek and I went to Long Island to visit them on Memorial Day weekend and, though Dan's color was a little off and his hair was thinning, he looked good. We sat in the dining room and spoke about his treatment, the diagnosis, and his plans while the kids were outside playing. He seemed to have a positive attitude and tried to make everyone feel at ease.

The next day they had a big barbeque, the kids swam in the pool, Dan's family and best friends were there, and we did our best ignore the fact that Dan was ill.

Before saying goodbye that day I gave him a big hug. He knew I was really worried about him and, in typical Danny fashion, told me, "Pat, don't worry. I'll be fine. They'll find a donor and I'll be okay."

"I know. But, I'm allowed to worry."

We agreed, but when we pulled out of the driveway I couldn't help but think that it could be the last time we saw him in the backyard cooking hamburgers, drinking a beer, and hanging out by the pool with the kids.

In the meantime, we had our own concerns about Derek's health. He was experiencing an inordinate amount of intense migraines and we wondered if his medications were to blame. Our family physician suggested we take him back to the neurologist who had originally prescribed Concerta and Wellbutrin, so an appointment was made.

I truly hated taking him there. Although the doctor was highly recommended and an expert in his field, he was less than thrilled spending his precious time with a young man who did not present full blown autism.

So when we returned my dander was up. I promised myself not to wimp out and merely accept his flippant remarks. I wanted to know whether the medication or something else was causing the headaches. By the end of the appointment Derek had prescriptions for a sleep-deprived EEG, a CBC live function test, a thyroid function test, Lyme disease tier, calcium, calcium magnesium and fasting blood sugar, together with an MRI.

While at work the next day, I called the hospital to schedule the EEG, the imaging facility for an MRI, and the diagnostic center for blood tests. As usual, I had to leave messages at each office and prayed that they'd return my calls when my boss was at lunch and not watching over my shoulder. Unfortunately, each time someone returned my call he was in his office within earshot and asked, "Pat, who is that?" I'd have to tell him the call wasn't for him, schedule the appointment quickly, and get off the phone before he walked near my desk.

The following week I took some time off to run Derek from one test to the other, then waited for the results. Every day I'd check my messages at home to see if we got a call from the doctor. I tried to convince myself that *no news is good news*, but I lost sleep at night worrying. By the second week I was anxious. I couldn't wait any longer and, at that point, didn't care whether my boss heard me call from the office.

"Hi. This is Pat Stroh, Derek Stroh's mother. I'm calling to see if you received the result of my son's tests."

"I'm, sorry," the receptionist said. "What is your son's name?"

"Derek Stroh."

"I need his date of birth."

"12/23/89."

"Please hold."

I listened to music for what seemed like an inordinate period of time and then heard a click. The connection was lost.

I called again.

"This is Pat Stroh. I was waiting to talk to someone about my son's test results and I got disconnected. Can you please forward me to the nurse?"

"Sure. What was your son's name again?"

"Derek Robert Stroh, date of birth 12/23/89."

I waited, and by the time my call was passed on to the nurse I felt my blood pressure rise.

"Mrs. Stroh, I'm sorry it took so long for me to pick up."

"That's okay. It's been a long time since my son completed the tests the doctor prescribed and I wonder whether you have the results?"

"Yes," she said. The EEG was negative for seizures. However, the EKG was abnormal with presence of bundle-branch block and inverted T-waves."

In other words, there was something wrong with his heart. I panicked. How long did they have the results? Why wasn't I contacted?

"I'm so sorry, Mrs. Stroh. I don't know why you weren't contacted. All I can suggest to you is that you contact your son's family physician for a referral to a pediatric cardiologist."

I slammed the phone down loud enough for everyone in the office to hear, then called our family practitioner's office for an appointment. Within a week we had the referral and the name of one of the best cardiologists in Albany.

Charlie and I took Derek up to Albany for his appointment. It was unnerving sitting in the waiting area not knowing what to expect. And, for a tense half an hour Charlie and I read magazines while Derek played his Gameboy. Then the door opened, a nurse called his name, and we were escorted to the back of the office where the EKG would be performed.

After the examination was complete, Charlie, Derek and I met with the doctor. He told us that there was a mild heart valve leak and that there would be no restrictions or limitations in activities and, in fact, encouraged dynamic activities because of his weight.

It would be our goal to have him lose 10-15 pounds by reducing his milk intake and substituting more nutritious snacks.

The doctor made arrangements for Derek to wear a Halter so that his heart rate could be monitored while he was actively participating in summer camp. He told us that if the results were good, he'd recommend that we repeat the Halter and echocardiogram in two years' time. So for the time being, Derek was to live his life as normal for the exception of more exercise, reduced milk intake, and a healthier diet.

Earlier in the year, Charlie and I made reservations for the house in Rhode Island and, considering it was closer to Irene and Dan than the Catskills, we decided to stick with our vacation plans. Perhaps vacationing at such a dire time was somewhat selfish, but we craved some time by the ocean.

Though Derek was getting older, he really didn't mind spending time with us on vacations. Charlie and Derek spent so much time in the waves that they would get water logged. We walked the beach, searched for shells and stones, ate clam cakes, and got a little burned.

One morning after locating our spot in the sand, the lifeguard warned that a pretty serious rip tide was detected. We watched as the life guards took their boards out and swam the length of the beach. It might be a little rougher than usual but they seemed to do just fine. We settled in, kept an eye on the waves, and started our day at the beach. Charlie got to work on a sand castle, Derek gathered large pieces of seaweed for me to save, and I dug my heels into the sand.

Worried about the undertow, Charlie and I were careful not to let Derek go out too far on his own. We spent a good deal of the day keeping an eye on him and calling him back to the beach when he got close to a crashing wave.

After lunch and a walk along the shore, Derek and Charlie went back in the water to jump through waves while I soaked up the sun. I watched some passing clouds and began to drift when, suddenly, I heard whistles blaring. I looked up and saw Derek cruising on top of a wave, but Charlie wasn't with him. I got up quickly and walked to the perimeter of the beach. Finally, I saw him in the distance. It was obvious the rip tide had him and he couldn't get back to shore. The lifeguards yelled at him to come in and I watched as Charlie fought the tide. Thankfully, with the help of a man who just escaped the undertow, he was able to swim to safety.

The rest of the vacation went well. We went back to the beach, played mini-golf, took a few trips into town, and hung out on the deck at night. Neither one of us wanted to go home, but it was time. We packed the car, hit the road, and headed back to the Catskills.

***

Unfortunately, Danny's health continued to deteriorate. Mom spent quite a bit of time traveling back and forth from Phoenicia to Long Island so she could watch the kids when Dan was in the hospital. Irene and I spoke as often as we could, but it was hard for her to break away.

The day she called to tell me that they found a transplant donor who was a perfect match, she was cautiously optimistic. He, or she, was from Italy and it would take quite a bit of coordination before the procedure took place, but she promised to keep me posted.

Mom agreed to stay on the Island until after the procedure knowing it could happen at any time and promised to keep me in the loop. There seemed to be a flurry of activity during the planning stage and it appeared that the transplant was imminent.

The phone rang at work and one of the secretaries yelled across the office, "Pat, I think it's your mom."

I grabbed the phone.

"Hello."

"Patty, it's Mom."

"Hi, are they taking him in," I asked.

"Bad news, hon."

"What?"

"The donor backed out."

"Are you kidding me? What do you mean, backed out? Now what?"

She explained that the doctors would have to find another donor but that they were running out of time.

I called Irene the next day and Dan answered the phone. I didn't know what to say, but tried to be positive.

"Dan, maybe there's a good reason the donor backed out. Maybe an accident or illness."

"I just can't believe there's a good reason. This is not good," he said.

Deep down, I knew he was right. But, I didn't want to end our conversation without trying to offer a glimmer of hope.

By the end of September, Danny's chances of recovery were diminishing. Another donor was found, but his doctor said he was too ill to have the transplant. With little time left, Dan and Irene flew up north to speak to a doctor who was willing to perform the transplant and we prayed for them. They were given some hope, but not long after their trip, Dan was admitted to the hospital. Mom stayed at Irene's so she could be at Dan's side. The news got increasingly worse; there was no positive news. So, we waited. I was at work when my mother called. "Danny's gone, Patti."

Danny's death was horrible. Irene loved him so much and did everything possible for him. He was a great man, father, husband and provider. Everyone that knew him loved him.

The funeral home was continually packed for three days and, while we were there, I watched Derek as he expressed his compassion. He'd walk up to Irene, not say anything, rub her back and place a kiss on her forehead. He sat next to Dan's mother and did the same. He didn't say much, as usual, just gave his cousins a hug.

Before the service, I sat next to Irene for a while. I took her hand and Derek stood behind and rubbed her back. She broke from her tears and said, "I can't believe this. This is the worst day of my life. I can't believe I'm burying my husband today. I just can't believe this."

None of us wanted to believe he was gone. We felt so bad for Irene and the kids and tried to say things to make them feel better, but there are no words to stop the flow of emotion when you lose someone so dear. Our hearts were sick and our minds were numb.

REALITY'S GREAT ESCAPE

Derek had done so well in eighth grade we were looking forward to ninth. This year he chose fashion design as an elective. When I questioned him about his choice he looked at me like I was crazy. It took a while for me to pull an answer out of him.

"Are you really interested in fashion design?"

He shrugged.

"Do you know what the class is going to be about?"

He looked at me, with eyebrows raised, and sighed, "Mom, I'm not stupid."

"So, you're going to design clothes, huh?"

"Well, I'm going to be the only guy in the class, and—"

I interrupted, "You're going to get a lot of attention from the girls."

"Duh," he replied.

About a month into the semester it was obvious that the consistency and perseverance of his middle school lead teacher was not going to be present in ninth grade. Although we heard nothing from the school, I could tell that Derek's enthusiasm had diminished. He became more resistant to the aides assigned to work with him and, though I did my best to encourage him to accept their help, I understood. He wanted friends and having an aide at his side did not help his social life.

He loved fashion design and was doing well in math because his teacher knew how to motivate him. Science was a struggle, but he seemed to be getting through. As always, English and History were his worst subjects and the teachers were less than enthusiastic to have him in their classes. In fact, his history teacher told us to consider calling in sick for the regent's exam because, "Kids like Derek don't pass."

Charlie and I worked with him on projects that included class presentations. He had no problem understanding the material. He knew what he read and amazed us with words of wisdom at the dinner table, but he stumbled when he had to speak in class. His speech was less than fluid and, at times, could be difficult to follow.

In frustration he'd ask, "Mom, what's wrong with me?"

It was extremely hard to watch his anger grow without having a clear answer. No one was ever able to explain why he had such difficulty and it was tormenting. We worked together researching subject matter, outlining appropriate information, writing an essay, and recording the presentation for him to play to the class.

Derek's sixteenth birthday was approaching fast and we wondered whether he was anxious to get a learner's permit. On one hand, Charlie and I were hesitant to allow him the privilege. On the other hand, we thought that having the freedom to visit friends and the mobility to look for work would broaden his social life.

One night during dinner, we discussed the possibility. "Dad and I are wondering if you want to go for your learner's permit."

"I don't think so," he replied.

"Come on, Dad said he'd be willing to teach you. Right, Charlie?"

"Duh, no. I'm not ready to drive."

By the end of the conversation, Charlie convinced him to at least read the driving manual.

Derek was content hanging out at the house as long as Raymond was over. He had no desire to expand his horizons. Unfortunately, his buddy got detention just before Christmas break and was unable to come over for Derek's birthday again. The pattern was getting old and I contemplated diversion.

I had already put a bug in Derek's ear so, when Raymond's mother called, it was as though skiing was the natural conclusion. Only this time, to our surprise, Charlie decided to join us. He preferred cross-country to downhill and on the occasion that the three of us were at Belleayre at the same time, he'd watch Derek ski from a view close to the lodge.

For a change, Derek's equipment went on like a charm and he was more than willing to give his dad a few pointers. After snapping our boots into the skis, it was time to head to the chairlift. As Derek gracefully swooshed down toward the lift I could see a look of pride on Charlie's face. And, by the time we were a quarter way down the mountain, he marveled at his son's balance and agility. A couple of times he yelled, "Derek, you're doing great."

There was a fresh coat of soft powder and it felt as though I was skiing on a cloud as I watched the reaction between the guys skiing ahead of me—each complimenting the other on their technique. We skied most of the day, stopping for an occasional snack, and all the way home Charlie repeatedly told Derek how proud he was of him. It was a gifted day.

***

The next day Derek and I finished making the last batch of our traditional holiday cookies. After the last batch was in the oven, he went back to his room to play a game and I began to prepare the gift baskets. Though chocolate chip cookies didn't reflect the season, they were easy to bake, less expensive, and good fillers on the bottom. So I grabbed that container from the freezer, pulled the lid off, and noticed that half of them were missing.

"Derek, get in here." He dragged himself away from the game and when he saw me looking in the containers, he knew he blew it.

I yelled, "What the hell did you do? Did you think I wouldn't notice? What am I supposed to do now?"

"Mom, I ate some cookies, I'm sorry, I didn't think I had that many. I'm a damn idiot. You probably hate me know."

He turned around, walked to his bedroom, and slammed the door and started to cry. What could I do? I took a deep breath, knocked on his door and signaled for him to meet me in my room. He shuffled, looking down at the floor as he followed me in. We sat on the bed for a few minutes, each thinking to ourselves. Then, I said, "Derek, I'm at a loss for words. What were you thinking?"

"I don't know," he groaned."

"Do you know how angry I am right now? Do you have any idea why I'm so angry?"

"Yeah, because you don't have enough cookies now."

"That's definitely part of it, but I'm worried about your health. You're eating too much again."

He shook his head and whispered, "I'm such an idiot."

"Look, kiddo. I can make smaller baskets, or bake more cookies, but I can't make a new you."

My anger turned to sadness. We hugged each other and he agreed to think about his health before eating all the cookies again.

Irene kept the kids on Long Island to share the holidays with Danny's family and I made dinner at home. Mom, Chet, Jess, Ed, Nikki, Faith, Dakota, Trudy and Charlie's cousin Warren, shared Christmas Day with us. After dinner, the kids ran around the house, playing games, and having fun. Derek absolutely loved his new game *Dance, Dance, Revolution* and spent most of his afternoon breaking a sweat.

Raymond showed up one day after Christmas and they spent their winter break together. And, although Derek held a bit of a grudge, all was forgiven as soon as he walked in the door.

New Year's was fast approaching and, as I reflected on Dan's death, I couldn't help but think that life was just too short to waste precious time. Trudy and I had been talking about a cruise and perhaps this was a good time for another escape.

Charlie wasn't at all interested and told me if I wanted to go with his mother, I'd have to take Derek, too. When I asked Trudy she was absolutely giddy and Derek was thrilled with the idea. Within a week, our trip to Florida, Nassau and the Bahamas on the Norwegian Dawn was booked for mid-March.

Trudy was so happy, she giggled every time was spoke about it. She shared her wardrobe choices with me. We shopped for bathing suits and sun hats together. She packed coordinating shoes for each outfit and made sure she secured the jewelry she'd wear for each occasion.

The morning of our departure, Charlie drove us to Rhinecliff and we took Amtrak to Penn Station. We arrived on time and grabbed a cab to the seaport where we got our first look at the Norwegian Dawn. Compared to Carnival's Jubilee, it was huge and I could only imagine that our cabin would be enormous.

We went through security, received our boarding passes, and made our way to the ship. The atrium was enormous. Black marble flooring lead to an elegant staircase which ascended to the shops above. After looking around for a while we took one of the glass enclosed elevators to Deck 9 and found our cabin. As soon as I opened the door it was obvious that my ability to visualize measurements was less than adequate. No doubt this was going to be a tight squeeze.

When the ship left port, Derek took off to check out the pool, buffet, and game room, and promised to meet us in the cabin before dinner. Trudy and I stayed on our balcony and watched as we passed the Statute of Liberty and the Verrazano Bridge, then we walked around the ship and outside to the pool area where it was a brisk thirtyish degrees.

That night the three of us went to the main dining room for dinner and discussed our plans for the night. Trudy and I decided to go to the casino to test our luck and Derek planned to find some teenagers to hang out with.

It was a long day and by the time I lost my first twenty dollars, I was ready to go to bed. Trudy was having a winning streak and would have stayed a bit longer but between the chardonnay and the movement of the ship, she was getting a little tipsy. It took a while to convince her to go to the cabin, but eventually she agreed. I wanted to find Derek so after I walked her to the cabin, I started my journey around the ship looking in the game room, the buffet area, and all the teen hangouts, but he was nowhere to be found. My main concern was not that he was up too late or spending too much money on video games, but that in an emergency I wouldn't be able to find him. I must have walked around for an hour before I checked back at the cabin. Both Trudy and Derek were watching TV and wondering where I was.

I was so tired I could hardly wait to go to bed, so while Trudy changed in the bathroom, I slipped on a night gown and Derek opened the sofa bed. It was then that I realized that his bed fit so snuggly between the queen sized bed and the balcony door that we couldn't go out to the balcony at night without climbing over him.

There I was: Derek on one side of me and Trudy on the other. We were like three sardines in a can. Minutes after saying goodnight Trudy fell asleep and started to snore. I laid as still as I could, listening to her deep bellowing sounds, thinking about what was about to transpire. As anticipated, Derek started to mimic her.

"Derek, you are going to have to deal with this. We can't control the fact that Grandma snores. I snore and you make noise, too. Please try to ignore the sounds and go to sleep." She continued to snore and his frustration grew.

He stamped his foot on the bed, grunted and said, "I can't take it. This sucks." I made him lay on his stomach, reached over and rubbed his back and head until he fell asleep. Before I knew it I was lying awake, eyes wide open, listening to both of them. At some point the ship rocked me to sleep.

***

The next morning Derek got up early and headed to the buffet for breakfast. By the time Trudy and I got there he was ready to make his way around the ship. We agreed to meet in the cabin around lunch time so that we could plan the rest of the day. I knew it would start getting warmer toward noon and the pool might be filled. After lunch we changed into our bathing suits and headed to the lido deck.

As soon as the protective nets came off and the staff gave the go ahead, Derek was in the pool. I watched as he checked out the other swimmers, saying hello to each of them. Then, proceeded to swim like a fish, diving under the water, doing hand stands and looking perfectly at ease.

"Come on in Mom, the water is great. You'll love it."

While we swam together he slipped me a hug. I rubbed his bristly blonde head and went back to my lounge chair. By that time the sun was pretty impressive and the daily drink special was looking mighty good. Derek came out of the pool when he heard us order a couple Pina coladas and ordered a virgin one for himself. There we were, the three of us, soaking up the sun with a cold drink in our hands, on a cruise ship, heading for Florida. Life was good.

After dinner we synchronized our watches and agreed to meet in the cabin no later than 11:00. Derek took off for parts unknown and Trudy and I went to the theater to watch a show. On the way back to the cabin we stopped to listen to a piano player for a little while, then ran into Derek in the hallway. That night was a repeat of the night before: Trudy snored, Derek got angry, and I did my best to appease him. What a joy!

The next morning wasn't any better. Trudy got on his nerves and he had no problem conveying it. She was getting a little tired of hearing him complain, and I was getting a little tired of playing referee. Perhaps a day in port would smooth things over.

Trudy had her heart set on an airboat adventure in Cape Canaveral. She had visions of gliding through the water in search for alligators and bald eagles, but it was sold out. We settled on a sightseeing cruise in search of dolphins, manatees, and different types of birds. It was a lazy day filled with wonderment and seemed to quell our nerves.

The next day we docked in Miami. I had booked a dolphin swim at the Seaquariam months before the trip and couldn't wait for the day to arrive. Before we left that cabin in the morning, I made sure Derek had his boarding/security card with him so we wouldn't have a problem getting back on the ship. We had a quick breakfast and the three of us headed down to the line of passengers waiting to disembark.

As the line began to move I reached into my pocket for my card. It wasn't there. I looked in every pocket of my backpack and didn't find it. I began to panic. I couldn't possibly go back to our cabin nine decks up, find my card, and get back to the line on time.

I told Trudy and Derek to get off the ship, go to the bus, and beg the driver to wait. Then, I ran back to the main desk, practically in tears, and hysterically exclaimed, "I booked an excursion to swim with the dolphins and the bus is about ready to leave. I don't have my ID card. Please help me."

The woman behind the desk looked at me as though I had lost my mind.

"Why didn't you bring your card? Where is your room?"

"We're on the 9th floor."

"Why can't you get it from your room?"

"There's no time, the bus is leaving any minute."

She looked at me with disgust, shook her head and sighed, "I can't believe this."

At that point I could feel my blood pressure rise.

"Look, I left the card in my room because I deeply wanted to plead with you to help me. I need a copy of my ID card and I need it now."

With a card in hand, I quickly got through security and ran to the bus. When I got on, the bus driver closed the doors and we were off. I felt as though everyone on the bus was watching me as I made my way through the isle. They must have thought I was crazy.

As soon as I sat down, Derek put his arms around me and said, "It's okay Mom. Good thing you found your card."

When we arrived at the Seaquarium, Trudy and Derek set off to take in the sights and I went to the classroom to attend a crash course on dolphin physiology and behavior with about ten other people. Afterwards, we put on wetsuits, met the trainer by the pool, got dolphin kisses, handshakes, and a short dorsal pull.

A half hour later I met up with Trudy and Derek at the dolphin show and watched *my* dolphin perform tricks. It was a great experience and one I wanted to repeat.

Our next stop was Nassau. We chose not to go to Paradise Island but to go to the local garden and zoo. In retrospect, Paradise Island would have been a lot more fun. But Trudy adored walking through the gardens, pinching off flowers and hiding them in her purse, while I turned red with embarrassment. And, if her thievery wasn't enough, Derek's imitation of each bird call was about all I could take. To no avail I begged the two of them to behave. On the way back to the bus, Derek walked with his arm around his grandmother as they cawed and giggled with excitement. I made believe I didn't know them.

I looked forward to our last stop before heading home. Norwegian's private island looked fantastic and, after the last two excursions, I was really looking forward to a day at the beach. That morning we got up early, waited for the tandem boat, and were the first to arrive. Trudy hated sand in between her toes and wanted nothing to do with the water, so after she was set up with a lounge chair and umbrella, Derek and I jumped in. The water was crystal clear and within seconds we were surrounded by amazingly vibrant colored tropical fish like we had seen in St. Thomas. He begged me for snorkeling gear and, though my money was running out, I agreed.

Derek was in his glory chasing after fish, Trudy was sipping on the early morning drink special, and I decided to take a walk along the beach's edge. I wandered toward the T-shirt hut where I charged a few souvenirs for everyone back home.

On my way back, I noticed that Derek was swimming without the snorkels. "Derek, where's the snorkel gear? I want to use it for a while."

"I turned it in. I saw the fish and I was finished with it."

"Did you think to ask if I wanted to use it," I replied.

He shrugged and gave me one of his *oh shit I'm in trouble* looks.

"Do you remember which guy you gave the gear to?"

He shrugged again.

"Get out of the water and follow me."

I marched him back to the hut to see if he could point out the person he returned the gear to, but he couldn't.

Again, Derek got a lecture about thinking before he acted while the steam from my ears slowed down to a trickle. As we walked back to the chairs he grabbed my hand, glared into my eyes with a frown on his face, rubbed my back, and apologized for not thinking.

There's never a dull moment or a day without a lesson. I shook my head, gave him a hug, motioned for him to follow me, and the two of us ran toward the water. We swam for quite a while before Trudy motioned us in. It was time to return to the ship.

That afternoon we left for New York and, within a day and a half, we were cruising up the Hudson toward the pier.

Before disembarking we reflected on our journey. No doubt the flowers pressed between pages in one of Trudy's books would remind her of our time together. I loved my time with the dolphins, swimming in the ocean, and the entertainment. Derek couldn't decide whether he liked the ocean, the pool, the shows, or the unlimited ice cream the most. But, the one thing we all agreed upon was if we were ever to go on a cruise together again, we'd need to book a bigger cabin.

FINDING A PLACE

After the vacation I was ready to take on the district and was hell bent to find a school Derek would thrive in. He was making it through ninth grade with a lot of modifications and advocacy, but he was reaching an educational cliff. In tenth grade his modifications would be so drastic that it hardly made sense for him to show up. On the other hand, there wasn't much out there for a kid who was consistently in the middle. We visited quite a few schools in the area and Derek's favorite was one was so liberal he could skateboard or play videogames all day until he felt like taking a class. This was not an option I was willing to pursue.

The Catholic school wasn't sure they had the support he needed and the private schools were so expensive we couldn't afford to send him. Someone suggested we consider one away from home. But as much as I wanted him to have the best education possible, I was not willing to send him away.

Just prior to the CSE meeting one of his teachers suggested that the only tenth grade program available to him would be the technical school's version of "life skills."

I was infuriated. I envisioned him sitting in a class sewing beads, baking cookies, and washing clothes. He could teach those classes and he was not going there.

At the meeting we discussed other options and decided to keep him in the high school as long as the teachers gave him their support and he accepted their help. As soon as he completed tenth grade he'd be able to start a half day program at the technical center at BOCES which would fit his educational needs. We developed a program for the following year and began contemplating a technical course of study for eleventh grade.

After a week of staying home alone during summer break Derek was ready to find work. The job had to be within walking distance. Our little community did not offer a lot, but there were a few stores. Thankfully, he got the nerve to ask the manager of the local grocery store if they needed help and he was handed an application. We worked together to fill it out and had a long discussion about the reason for supplying a social security number. The next day I drove him down to the store, he handed in the application, and a new life's lesson began. He had never thought about the employment process before and thought the job was his. He was surprised that he wasn't called immediately and became increasingly upset as each day that passed.

Finally, he called me at work and said, "Mom, I got the job. I'm going to work part time." I was so happy I let out a little scream, asked him when he was going to start, how many days he'd be working, and what his schedule would be. He replied, "Whoops, I didn't ask ... maybe tomorrow?"

I drove him down to the market later that day, reminded him of our planned vacation to Rhode Island, and sent him in with a calendar. Within a few minutes he ran back to the car and told me he'd be working about three days a week from 3:00 p.m. until about 8:00 p.m.

He started work the following week, fronting shelves, and bringing in grocery carts from the parking lot. The kids that worked there welcomed him and, by the end of the week, I could tell he was happy. His first pay check was a small one but he was absolutely thrilled.

After a few weeks of repeatedly fronting shelves and bringing in carts, he started to get a little bored. Charlie and I did our best to keep a positive momentum going, hoping our vacation would help break the monotony.

Derek was thrilled that Raymond was coming along and more than willing to blow the money he earned on the two of them. I watched for hours as they jumped into the waves. Derek was in his element and Charlie loved spending time with him. Raymond sat back a bit and spent a lot of the day fighting a sunburn. He liked the ocean, but not as much as Derek.

Our friends Annette and Greg drove down to spend some time with us and on our last day we decided to sit in a different area on the beach. After setting up our blankets, Raymond took his place in the sand. Derek begged him to go in the water, but he didn't want to go in.

Derek yelled to Charlie, "Come in, Dad" and ran into the waves. Charlie looked at Raymond and the rest of us, shrugged his shoulders, turned toward the ocean, ran through the water, and dove through a wave. A few seconds later I watched as he stood up holding his head. Something was wrong.

I walked toward him and saw blood pouring down his face. I yelled for a life guard and people started to gather around as he got closer to shore. He looked pretty shook up and said when he dove into the wave he hit a rock with his head. The lifeguards wanted to get a stretcher and take him from the beach to the boardwalk but he'd have no part of it. He would walk to the boardwalk and, only then, would he let them take him by ambulance to the hospital.

Annette and Greg stayed with the guys and I followed the ambulance. As soon as I saw him in the emergency room I knew he was going to be fine. They put a few *staples* in his head and sent us on our way.

We went back to the beach and stayed for a while but, the smell of the salt water, feel of the sand between our toes, and roar of the waves were less exciting. We left Rhode Island the next day and Raymond went home to recoup from a week with the Stroh's.

Derek went back to work fronting shelves at the supermarket and saved enough money to buy a Play Station II and a few games he desperately wanted. Unfortunately, not long afterwards the thrill of the job wore off. He got tired of the repetition and spent more time in the bathroom hiding than doing his work. He lost the bounce in his step as he left the store and I knew the gig was up. One day the manager told me it wouldn't be long before they let him go.

Charlie and I thought it would be best if he left the job before he was fired. So, when he said, "I think I'm going to have to spend a lot of time on school work this year. Maybe I should quit when school starts," we agreed.

He had to do well in tenth grade. It was his ticket to technical school. I had finally given up emotionally and intellectually any hope of changing his program to a local or regents program. He'd have to work extremely hard, be totally committed, and motivated. But, he wasn't.

Unfortunately, Raymond was transferred to BOCES for the entire school day and Derek was having a difficult time socializing with the kids at school. He was either ignored or bullied while walking through the hallways and came home tormented.

At the end of each school day he'd call me at work,

"Hi, Mom, I'm home."

"How was school?"

"Okay."

"Do you have any homework?"

"No. Can we go to Kingston? I want a new game."

"Hon, it's been a long day."

"Please, Mom. I really want this game."

"Not today."

He'd hang up and I'd start to worry. I couldn't give in all the time, but I was afraid of his response. His frustration and anger were beginning to build and he'd take it out on the molding, a fixture, or a piece of furniture. He was alone. He wanted more of a life than the one he had with me and Charlie. He was a young man in body and spirit, but lacked the social nuances to be able to connect with peers. The old ABDCEFG disorder didn't afford him the ability to speak his mind as quickly as others and it was driving him crazy.

Thankfully, he had two teachers who were extremely good for him and willing to help him as much as they possibly could. To our amazement he passed both his math and science regents competency tests. I was so proud of the work he had done that I called the entire family. Again, my mind wandered. Perhaps if we kept him in the intensive classes he could graduate with a local degree.

I was sure the teachers and social worker at school thought I was crazy. I spent so many hours communicating with them trying to figure out what to do. I was so confused. We worked hard to be sure that Derek got the best education possible and I wanted him to grow up, get a job he liked, and live a happy life.

As usual, I tossed and turned at night trying to figure out the best path. I had to be sure that the goals we set could be met. I was so excited that he did well on the tests that I couldn't help but think that we might be selling him short. No one had the answers: not the educators, psychologists, counselors, and especially not me.

One morning I woke up questioning who I was fighting for. Was it for Derek or me? After years of advocating for him, I now had to figure out what the best education was. How important was it for my son to have a regents or local degree? Would it look better on paper? Would it give him the opportunity to be admitted to a secondary school? What options between life skills and college were there? So many years were spent negotiating through each CSE meeting, IEP, annual and tri-annual review. How or when do I give in?

At times I just wanted to say the hell with it. All the pressure was too much, but I didn't. I kept the notion of regents, local, and IEP diplomas at bay. For the time being we would move on as planned.

In the meantime, I had to wrap myself around the fact that my little boy was turning seventeen. When I was his age I was a hellion. My parents had been divorced for two years, each married new spouses, and I became rebellious. I started hanging out with a bunch of people who went to anti-war demonstrations, was part of a sit in at the local draft board, marched in the Kent State Moratorium, and spent *May Day* in D.C. screaming "Hell no, we won't fight this fucking war." Poor Jessica had to endure an entire week of the Democratic Convention when she was seven and Derek had to listen to me rant and rave about the Iraq War.

A month or so before our president was elected for a second term Derek came running into the living room, "Mom, I came up with a great slogan: *If George Bush Is Our Future, We're History.*" Not only did it confirm that he was listening to me, but he made the connection. A few days later I ordered bumper stickers and figured out how to make buttons. Some of his teachers loved the idea and proudly displayed his slogan on their cars.

Needless to say, I was glad he got it. Understanding a bit of politics and being self-expressive was important and I was thrilled. He never turned down a chance to go to New York and join a protest with me.

On the lighter side, winter was upon us and we took advantage of our town's ski program at Belleayre just about every weekend. Derek was skiing wonderfully, turning and swooshing down the mountain so quickly I couldn't keep up.

Nikki skied straight down screaming, "Grandma you're so slow, hurry up or I'm going to beat you down the hill."

When she fell; I'd be sure she was all right before I passed her yelling, "I'm going to beat you down the hill, you're so slow!"

Derek waited for Nikki on the lift line and the two of them rode together while I got matched with a single. Sometimes, from two chairs away, I could see him torment her and she'd scream, "Grandma, make him stop."

After a couple seasons of listening to her screech, I'd yell back, "I can't hear you, I have my helmet on."

Most of the time they'd get off the lift laughing, directing which trail we'd ski down, and how they'd beat me to the bottom.

Except for the seating and the occasional chairlift argument, skiing was wonderful. I thoroughly enjoyed watching the kids as they made their way down the mountain and, though Derek was not particularly thrilled about dropping Raymond off at home to spend time with Nikki and me on Sunday mornings, he loved it after we got going.

The last day of skiing was a little warmer than usual and the snow was packed to perfection. Just before our last run, I asked the kids to wait before they raced down the hill. They reluctantly waited for me to catch up with them.

"Listen guys, I just want to tell you how happy I am that we can ski together.

Let's make this last run special, okay?"

Derek motioned and blew me a kiss and Nikki screeched, "I love you Gram."

Derek led the way, Nikki followed his ski trail, and I followed hers. As I watched them glide down the mountain ahead of me, I felt sheer joy. While we packed our gear and headed home, I wondered how much longer we'd ski together. Only time would tell.

Derek was somewhat happy that ski season was over since Raymond could stay over every weekend from Friday to Sunday afternoon. Mostly, they played video games, took an occasional walk, made swords, and had battles in the house when Charlie and I weren't home. And, the weekends that Raymond couldn't come over, he was miserable.

Late spring we were invited to BOCES to attend the presentations conducted by the technical classes. I thought he might be interested in the culinary because he had an affinity for food, but he wanted to take computer repair. He was well on his way to graduating tenth grade and we all agreed that computer technology was his destiny.

Unfortunately, he had nothing planned for the summer. So, before the school year ended, I called and spoke to his counselor and lead teacher to see if they had any information regarding work study programs. They had nothing.

I called mental health and spoke to our friends at Kids Together, but they had nothing, either. I called a variety of agencies and Derek was either too high functioning or not high functioning enough for any of the programs available.

I was worried about him. Raymond was going to attend summer school to bring his grades up and no one responded to his job applications.

I sat in my therapist's office explaining my frustration and she suggested I check out summer camps. She thought it would be a good experience for him and would give me some freedom from the day to day work and concern for his wellbeing. By the end of my session I was convinced that camp would be a great idea.

At dinner that night, I spoke to the guys about my therapist's suggestion. Neither one of them was impressed with the idea. But, when I promised Derek that he'd be home from camp before Raymond was finished with summer school, he reluctantly agreed to think about it.

The next day I got on the phone with counselors, the special education department at school, and mental health department, to locate a viable camp situation for him. If he was less functioning or higher functioning we wouldn't have a problem. If we had $15,000 he could start the week after school ended. Again, nothing was available for my kid in the middle. I got online and started checking every possible link I could.

After days of searching I found a six week program about half an hour away. When I spoke to the director he seemed very much in tune with my needs and explained that, because of Derek's functioning level and age, he could be enrolled as an intern in training. He'd be assigned an age appropriate mentor who'd take him under his wing and together they would help the less functioning kids. It sounded promising and we agreed to visit the camp after our return from our family trip to Florida.

Patricia Stroh

***

Our plans had been solidified for a while. Trudy was more than willing to take the next journey with us, so I did quite a bit of research trying to find a place in the Florida Keys that would accommodate the four of us. After showing everyone the brochures and information from online searches we all agreed to go to Islamorada. The hotel we picked had a very large suite with two bedrooms, a couch that opened in the living room, and a full kitchen. There was a salt water pool, fresh water pool, restaurant and bar on site and, if I booked it in time, we could get the suite closest to the ocean.

After years of coordinating vacations and learning a bit from my miscalculations, I learned what to expect and how to make the trip less hectic. I booked a non-stop flight to Miami, a good sized rental car, and a hotel near the airport to stay at the night before our flight.

Our plane was a bit smaller than we were used to and the TV hovering over us on the ceiling rattled on takeoff, but it was a decent flight. We caught a shuttle to our rental car and made it to Islamorada just before check in time. The hotel was everything I expected and more.

The Islander Resort was the perfect oceanfront location. With its blend of oceanfront elegance and casual island atmosphere, it was perfect. The pools were beautiful and the view of the ocean from the tiki bar and restaurant were stunning.

We spent the first couple days enjoying the view, hanging out by the pool, sipping rum drinks, and soaking in the sun. We went to *Theater by the Sea* which, of course, had dolphin encounters. I got the chance to swim in a deep lagoon alongside them and spent a lot more time in the water than I did in Miami, so I was thrilled.

Toward the end of our vacation Trudy and I begged the guys to go to Key West with us. Neither of them wanted to go, but after enough nagging they agreed. Unfortunately, we picked a day when the heat and humidity was so oppressive neither of us could breathe. Trudy and Derek were miserable and I wished I hadn't been so insistent.

Overall, we had a very nice time together and I felt as though the trip was a success, but Trudy decided that she wouldn't fly again and perhaps it was time for her to give up vacationing.

The following week I scheduled a meeting at the camp. Derek and I met the director and were introduced to the young man who he would be working with. We took a leisurely walk, viewed the cabins, walked through the cafeteria, and to the various buildings that incorporated computer workshops, arts and crafts, and a stage. The director brought us into a cabin and introduced us to about six boys. Out of all of the kids in the cabin, one looked up from a book, acknowledged our presence, and said hello to Derek. I noticed that one of the boys was having difficulty controlling his movements and appeared to be pretty low functioning. I asked why they were in the cabin in the middle of the afternoon and was told that the kids had free time to do whatever they wanted and that they chose to relax in their cabin.

I wasn't thrilled with the combination of kids and the look on Derek's face showed that he wasn't either. As we continued our walk through the camp I asked where Derek would be staying if we decided to register. He pointed to a group of cabins located away from the one we had just visited and told us that they were dedicated to interns — which is exactly what I wanted to hear.

The director explained to Derek that, as an intern, he would also be responsible to complete one job each day and, as a bonus, he'd be entitled to leave the premises with the other interns to go to the movies, to play mini-golf, or take in a movie.

He did all he could to convinced us that it would be a wonderfully uplifting experience and I fell for it — with one glaring exception. We would only be able to communicate by phone on Sundays. We could write each other as much as we wanted to and communicate via e-mail from the camp's computer, but the limitation of one telephone call a week was going to be difficult.

It was the first time he'd be away from us and six weeks seemed like an eternity. On the other hand, he *was* seventeen and needed to break away at some point. He'd be an intern, receive job skills, work with other kids less fortunate than him, and have the opportunity to leave campus once or twice a week. On the way home we talked about the healthy experience he'd have hiking, swimming, controlling his eating habits, the possibility of losing some weight and, before we pulled in the driveway, he agreed to go.

I did everything I could to make the prospect of camp an enjoyable one. I hyped it so much that it got ridiculous. We bought new clothes, hiking shoes, bathing suits and stationary. I put together a note book with his favorite *Anime* picture on it and did everything I could to make sure he would feel close to home. He had my e-mail at work and at home. He had Jessica's e-mail and everyone's address.

The first morning of camp we were met at the entrance by the kid who was slated to take Derek under his wing and he directed us to the welcome area. Charlie parked the car, Derek grabbed the suitcase and we walked up to the *so called* greeting committee. I noticed a lot of kids on the very low end of the spectrum, a couple of kids with Tourette's Syndrome, and knew we were in trouble. As a mom of a special needs kid I would be less than compassionate if I didn't accept these children as much as I expected others to accept my son. But, if Trudy's snoring was a problem on the ship, I could just imagine how hard it would be for him to be in a cabin with a kid with Tourette's. I searched out the director to confirm that Derek would be staying in the cabin with interns and he promised that he would.

The counselors asked that we make our goodbyes quick so the kids could adapt to the situation easier. We gave Derek a quick hug and kiss, cheered him on, and sent him on his way. I cried all the way home.

The director called me at work early that week to tell me that Derek was having difficulty and wanted to come home. He was not settling in well and thought if I talked to him I'd be able to convince him to stay. I agreed to try only if he was allowed to talk to me in private and, in a low, monotone voice he said, "Hi, Mom. I want to come home, I don't like it here. Please come and get me."

I missed him already and, though for a second I was ready to give in, I told him to stick it out until Sunday. "Derek, you're seventeen and have never been away from home, it's going to take a while to get used to. Please try to hook up with that kid you were introduced to. I promise we'll call you first thing Sunday morning."

He begrudgingly agreed to stay, we said goodbye, and tears started to well up in my eyes. It was a lot more difficult than I anticipated.

Sunday morning came and I called exactly at 9:00 a.m. as instructed. Of course, the phone was busy because every parent was instructed to call at that time. I hit the redial button for what seemed like an eternity and imagined Derek pacing in frustration. Finally, I got through and they transferred me to the cafeteria. He sounded a bit better than the last call but wasn't completely resolved. Yes, he still wanted to come home, but the interns were going to the bowling alley in a couple days. Besides, he made a friend of one of the young girls working in the office. It was a good sign. I promised to call him the following Sunday and we said our goodbyes.

A few days later I received an e-mail from the director. Derek was not doing well and he thought it might be a good idea if I talked to him again.

"Mom, I hate this place. I can't sleep. There's a kid in the cabin that keeps screaming at night. There's another one that tries to run away and go back home to Africa and I have to bring him back into the cabin. I hate it here. I want to come home."

"Derek, put the director on the phone."

I asked him what cabin Derek was in and he told me that there wasn't enough room in the interns' cabin, so he was placed in a cabin with one other intern and four other kids.

At that very second I wondered whether I should pull him from camp. Something had to be done because the situation was not acceptable.

We all agreed that Derek would be given earplugs and if he was still unable to sleep at night, he would be moved. He agreed to try, but asked if he might be able to come home a little earlier. We'd talk about it on Sunday.

Toward the end of the week we got a letter. He wrote that he missed us, but the interns were going mini golfing that week and,

"Hey, Mom. Get ready to see a new game you and I did not know about. I'll show you the name of it. It's called Tales of Legindia. You might not know what their saying. (Their speaking in Japanese [spelling mistake]). I need 20 more dollars from Dad. Love: Derek.

P.S.S. Would you put the money in with one of the letters please!!!"

After reading the letter I felt somewhat relieved and during our Sunday phone call he talked about a girl from Russia who danced with him. He told me that he was trying to convince the camp director to buy *Dance, Dance Revolution*. But again, he asked if he could come home early. I didn't know what to do. Charlie, Jessica, my Mom, and everyone at work told me not to give in. They thought I should enjoy my time without responsibility for a change, that he was old enough to deal with being away from home, and that this adjustment would be an accomplishment for both of us.

For the next two and a half weeks the letters and conversations continued. He would beg, I would convince him to stay, we would hang up, and I would cry. Toward the end of the six week session we received a letter:

"Mom, would you please pick me up on Thursday. I'm not kidding. I want to come home. I'm tired of this fucking place. Plus would you send me 20 more dollars. Please would you free me from this place? Please, Please. Love: Derek"

The next day I called him and explained that if he stayed a few more days, he'd be able to attend the closing ceremony and have his final dance with the Russian receptionist. But, he wanted no part of it. There was so much sadness in his voice, I prepared his escape.

I spoke to the director and advised him that I would be picking Derek up the next day. I got there about 10:50, walked toward the cabins and found him there. I reached out to him and he gave me a big hug and kiss, then whispered, "I thought you'd never come. Thanks for getting me out of this hell hole."

We walked to the car with our arms around each other as he dragged his suitcase behind. Though I thought he would have felt better if he made it through the end, I was thrilled to have him back.

That night before he settled into his newest videogame, he sat next to me on the couch and gave me hug. He told me how much he loved me and that he missed me so much that he'd cry himself to sleep every night.

I replied, "Me, too."

We were both relieved that it was over. There's no place like home.

SIMPLE PLEASURES

For the balance of the summer he stayed home and Raymond came over every Friday after school. They spent their time outside with their makeshift swords, swam in the pool, or were glued to a videogame. Every Friday was pizza night and, when the weather was right, Charlie put together a fire in the back. Sometimes we roasted marshmallows, listened to creepy stories, or to Charlie playing guitar. When the fire died out, Charlie and I went to bed and the guys stayed up.

Regardless of the time spent sleeping, Derek would get up early Saturday mornings to put the coffee on and wait for me to walk into the kitchen. I'd get a big bear hug, a crack of my aching back, and a kiss good morning. And, as soon as I filled my cup with coffee, walked into the living room, and put the news on, he'd plop himself on the couch next to me.

This morning before the first sip of coffee hit my lips he started, "Mom, we really, really want to see a movie. Can you take us to Kingston?"

"Aw, come on, Derek. Can you wait until I finish my coffee before you bug me?"

I had been working in the office all week and wanted to stay home, work in the yard, pick some blackberries, jump in the pool, and eat outside for dinner. I didn't want to drive to Kingston.

"Seriously, Derek. Get a job and get your license. I'm so tired of going to the mall every Saturday afternoon. It's too nice out to waste my day in Kingston."

He shot me his innocent pout and, as usual, I agreed.

I got my second hug of the morning and he ran into his bedroom to wake Raymond. Derek screamed, shook the bed, stamped his feet, and finally I heard him stir. Within a half an hour Raymond dragged his extremely tall teenage body off the top bunk of the bed, got dressed, and slowly made his way to the car.

On our way to Kingston Derek and I sang to a Dave Matthews CD while Raymond curled up in the back seat sound asleep. Miraculously, he woke up when I pulled into the mall parking lot. I dropped them off and did some shopping until it was time to pick them up. They came out laughing hysterically and I got the entire story line on the way home. By the time we pulled in the driveway, the afternoon was practically over.

This pretty much sums up the remainder of the summer. Raymond showed up on Friday afternoons and either his dad picked him up, or I'd drive him home around noon on Sundays. Derek and I took advantage of the rest of the day swimming in the pool. He'd dunk me under a couple of times and spend an inordinate amount of time practicing handstands. When Charlie joined us, I officiated handstand contests.

On one hand I was relieved that he was comfortable at home with us. On the other hand, I was haunted by his inability to develop socially. He needed to do things that seventeen year old guys did. By then he stood six inches taller than me, had gorgeous blue eyes, and spiked white blonde hair and a lot of whiskers. He dressed like a "Goth" and, though I wasn't thrilled with spots of black nail polish on his bedroom's ocean blue floor, I didn't mind his style at all. If his clothes gave him a sense of belonging, so be it.

As was our tradition, I drove him to school the first day. Usually he'd sneak a kiss to me before getting out of the car. This time he said goodbye in a monotone voice, got out of the car, and slid me a quick wave behind his back. I watched as my guy in black walked through the doors. Admittedly, I missed my kiss, but he was maturing and did exactly what he needed to do.

When he called me at work after school that afternoon he seemed like a different person. He told me that he met a few kids from Kids Together at BOCES, got a hug from his old crush, LeeAnne, and was very happy with the computer class.

Sometime after the second week I got a call from his math teacher. She was concerned that an aide wasn't assigned to Derek and thought that he might have difficulty without one. I was adamantly opposed to an aide and explained that during his annual meeting, it was agreed that we'd do anything to avoid that scenario during his BOCES classes. At seventeen he was wary of being told what to do and resisted any connection, conversation, or lecture from anyone other than a teacher.

Besides, computer tech was something that he might be able to excel at without someone constantly breathing down his back. I wanted him to have a fresh start and feared he might be ridiculed or ostracized by a new group of kids. It was agreed; no aide at BOCES.

We went to the open house during the first semester and, for a change, the teachers were impressed. Not only was he successful in his computer class, but he was excelling in English and math as well. We spoke with a representative from a state funded program who indicated that they might be able to find Derek a job the following summer. And, they would train him during his senior year to prepare him for the job market.

I left that night believing that life *was* going to be better for him. I envisioned him sitting in an office, working on computers, meeting friends for lunch, and taking home a pay check. I went so far as to imagine him picking up his girlfriend, driving to the beach, falling in love, finding an apartment, getting married, and having children.

I wondered how I'd be able to handle all of that. I'd miss him so much. Who'd sing with me in the car or greet me at the door? It would be very difficult for me, but this was the plan all along. I wanted nothing more than for him to be independent, to have a family, and to be happy. Now, I wasn't sure I'd be able to handle his independence with grace.

He passed the first semester with flying colors. Every once in a while he'd get home from school and practice a new computer repair technique. Sometimes he'd screw up the program and Charlie had to fix it, but he was learning.

Just after the second semester started, I took Derek up to Albany for his scheduled appointment with the cardiologist. As usual, the doctor didn't seem concerned with his overall health, but he was not happy with his weight gain. He tried to impress upon Derek the importance of exercise. Skiing and swimming was not enough and suggested that walking back and forth from school might be a good idea. He prescribed a 24 hour monitor to test his heart rate and told me he'd contact me after he received the results.

On our way home we spoke about the doctor's suggestion and, though walking back and forth to school seemed like a good idea, Derek was less than thrilled. The hill below our house was extremely steep and difficult to climb. In fact, well trained bicyclists and runners had difficulty getting to the top. I, with a mild case of asthma, had to stop several times before reaching the driveway and understood his dilemma. Before we got home it was agreed that he'd exercise a half hour each day with his *Dance, Dance Revolution Game* and walk to school in the morning.

A week after the halter was sent back for evaluation, I received a call from the cardiologist. He was somewhat concerned about the test results because it appeared that Derek's heart rate had increased a bit that night. I questioned Derek about his activities that evening and he reminded me that he was exercising with the game.

The next day I called the doctor and, though the doctor thought it might be a reason for the increased heart rate, he wanted us to return in six months.

Raymond continued to show up most Friday afternoons even though he was getting a little tired of the repetition. I could tell that he had little desire to play a dance game, but he did at Derek's insistence. Mostly, after dinner they'd hang out in the bedroom to watch TV or play videogames.

Winter began to descend upon us and the cold air was less than pleasant. Raymond came over Friday night and, after the dance marathon, they had dinner and went back into the bedroom for most of the night. The next morning Derek got up early and once again begged me to take them to Kingston. It was cold outside and I just wanted to stay home, do some housework, sit in the hot tub, and enjoy the day off.

"Ah, Derek. Do we have to go in to Kingston again? Can't you guys do something else for a change," I asked.

"Well, Mom, what would you say if I was named student of the month? And, did I mention that I made honor roll at BOCES?"

"Are you kidding me," was my reply.

I asked him if he had anything to prove he had attained this great accomplishment and to my amazement he pulled out an award from his backpack.

"Go wake Raymond up. We're going to Kingston," I told him.

While I waited for the guys to get dressed and ready to go, I grabbed the award and brought it back into our bedroom to show Charlie. Then,

I called my mother, Jessica, Trudy, and Irene with the good news. It may have seemed like a small achievement for him to receive the Student of the Month Award and to be on honor roll for a few BOCES classes to some, but to me it meant the world.

As I drove down the highway, I tapped him on his knee and told him how proud I was. We sang all the way to Kingston while Raymond slept in the back.

WINTER'S WRATH

Unlike Thanksgivings in the past, we decided to go to a local restaurant for dinner. Usually, Irene would bring the kids and their dog from Long Island and we'd congregate at my mother's house for dinner. However, my mother's husband, Chet, had been in and out of the hospital for a while and we thought that it might be too much for him to have the kids and dog run around.

Though the buffet dinner was fine, it just didn't have the ambiance of barking dogs, screaming kids, and the usual family insanity. Our table was long, which made it difficult to communicate with one another, and I had little time to talk to Irene.

Not long after Thanksgiving, Chet was admitted to a cancer ward. Mom stayed with him day in and day out. And on Saturdays, when the boys were at the movies, I went to visit for as long as I could emotionally handle it. I could tell that Chet wasn't going to be with us for too much longer, but Mom was the consummate optimist. She hand fed him with the hope he'd be home for Christmas.

Derek turned eighteen December 23, 2007. I reflected on the past and was relieved that he was showing signs of maturity.

Raymond, who had either been sick or grounded on Derek's previous birthdays, made it to this one. I drove them to Kingston for a movie in the afternoon and later that day Charlie and I took them to a Mexican restaurant in Woodstock. Birthday cake followed at home and the guys were back in the bedroom.

After Raymond went home in the morning, Derek and I went to the hospital to visit with Chet and Mom. Chet wasn't going home for Christmas so Mom decided to stay in the hospital with him. She decorated the window with a wreath and placed a little Christmas tree on his bed stand. She was a trooper. She loved that man so much and, whether he was cognitively aware or not, she was not going to leave him.

Not long after we got there the doctor peeked his head in and Mom left the room to speak to him. It was extremely difficult to sit in the room and watch Chet suffer. He was weak, barely able to speak, and in and out of consciousness. After a few minutes, Derek and I walked back into the family room where we met Mom. She was sitting at the table with her hands covering her face and it was obvious that the doctor didn't give her the news she longed for.

We approached her quietly. I sat down next to her and Derek stood behind her. He rubbed her back and kissed the top of her head as she sat crying. He spoke to her tenderly with an awareness that overwhelmed me. Over the years he developed an ability to express compassion for people in pain. Perhaps it was his reaction to Charlie's bicycle accident, or that he had endured enough loss to be deeply touched.

I made Christmas dinner for the kids, Trudy and Charlie's cousin Warren. As usual, Derek loved his presents and spent half the day playing videogames and hanging out with the kids. Charlie and I decided that our Christmas gift to each other would be the Holiday Inn New Year's Eve package that included a room for the night, a buffet, and a lot of dancing.

Since Derek had shown definite signs of maturity, we agreed to his request that he and Raymond be able to stay home alone while we were away. Raymond's parents didn't have a problem with it and the guys promised we wouldn't come home to a mess.

Before leaving for the hotel, I made sure that the phone number was strategically placed on the refrigerator and that they knew how to get a hold of us in an emergency. Jessica and Ed were staying home with the kids and they promised to be available in the event the guys needed them. Derek, Raymond and Charlie thought I was being over protective and teased me until it was time to go.

It wasn't until we reached the hotel and settled into our room that I started to relax. After I called Derek to give him the room number, Charlie and I went to the pool and sat in the hot tub and sauna for a while. Then we got dressed for the party.

Though Charlie wasn't in his comfort zone sitting with people we didn't know, we had a great meal, unlimited drinks, and danced to just about every song. By mid-night, Charlie's jacket and tie were thrown over the back of his chair and I was dancing barefoot.

While we celebrated the New Year, a snow storm approached from the west. When we woke up that morning there was about a foot of snow on the ground. After breakfast and a couple cups of coffee we left for home. While we inched our way back in blizzard conditions, I wondered what kind of mess the guys had made that night. But, to our surprise, they did fine.

By mid-January it was evident that Chet wasn't going to bounce back. Even though he was fading fast, Mom held on to the hope that he'd survive. Toward the end of the month his doctor explained that there was nothing left for them to do so he was admitted to a local nursing home. Mom continued to watch vigil over him in the hope he would gain strength, but on February 1, 2008, he passed away.

Mom lost the love of her life and I wasn't sure how to console her. What do you say when a person dies? How do you make those who remain feel better? I just didn't know how to handle my mother's pain. I called her often, had her for dinner, and did the best I knew how, but I wasn't Chet.

The early part of winter was brutally cold and miserable. Derek was less enthusiastic about skiing, so Nikki and I went a couple of times without him. But, I hesitated to go when the thermometer read less than 30° and refused to leave the house when it was a blustery 14°. Just the thought of sitting on a chairlift in the wind and cold was bad enough, but the lifts had a tendency to breakdown in the cold.

Even the thought of going to work in the morning made me shiver. I wished I had one of those remote car starters to warm it up. It would have been great if I could turn it on and warm it up so that the ice would simply melt off the windshield, but I had a standard transmission so, that luxury was not an option.

One morning my car just didn't want to start. It took forever to warm up and, of course, I got to work a few minutes late. As usual, my boss was in the conference room waiting for me to deliver him his newspaper and when I walked in the door he glanced at his watch. He never understood how difficult it was for me to drive to work in the winter. His house was within walking distance of our office, but I had to drive down windy, country roads in lousy conditions and, at times, feared for my life.

I knew he'd be watching the clock when I went to lunch so I decided to stay in and not give him the chance to say something to me. Besides, it was frigid outside and I had no real intentions of leaving.

Not long after my boss left the office to walk home, the phone rang. It was Charlie's boss' secretary. By the sound of her voice, I knew something had happened. She quickly told me that Charlie had an accident at work. He fell off a second story deck and was in the cold for a while. She wasn't sure how it happened or how he was, but he was taken by ambulance to Kingston Hospital. I tried to get more information from her, but she had nothing. As soon as we hung up I grabbed my purse and rushed upstairs to tell the other secretary that I had to leave and would call her when I knew more.

As I drove to the hospital all the feelings and fears I had the day he was hit came crashing back. But, at least then, I knew he was alive. This time, I had no idea. My thoughts raced as I made it closer to Kingston and wondered what I'd see when I walked into the emergency room. When I got the hospital I grabbed the first parking spot and ran to the entrance. A security guard walked me to the emergency room, found a nurse, and she brought me to Charlie. Thank god he was conscious and talking to the doctors when I stepped in the room. I walked as close as I could to the bed while they checked his vitals and looked at his injuries. He looked at me, shook his head, and began to sob.

"Charlie, what happened?"

"You won't believe it, he groaned. I fell from a second story deck."

As the doctors poked and prodded, he told me that he was working outside on the deck when the door into the house locked. His cell phone was in the truck, and the house was isolated in the woods. There was no one around and it was freezing out. So, he looked down from the deck and decided he could climb over the railing, shimmy himself half way down, and jump to the ground. Unfortunately, when he stepped over the railing and started his descent, the railings gave way. He fell, landing directly on the railroad ties below. He screamed in pain while he tried to pull himself toward the house. He wondered how long it would take for someone to find him and whether he would freeze to death before he was found. And, if it wasn't for a neighbor returning from vacation and checking his mail box that particular moment, no one would have heard his screams.

Before the lab technicians came to wheel him out for x-rays, one of the doctor's pulled me aside and said, "Mrs. Stroh, we are sure that *Spiderman* has broken his ribs in quite a few places and most likely has a collapsed lung."

As soon as he was taken to radiology, I called Jessica to tell her what had happened and asked her to stop by the house after school was out to tell Derek. Then, I waited for quite a long time, pacing in the emergency room and the lobby before the nurse came to get me.

When I walked back into the emergency room the doctor told me that Charlie, in fact, had several broken ribs and had a collapsed lung. I watched as an intern tried to insert a stint while Charlie screamed in pain. Meanwhile, the nurses went to work getting an IV in place and doing their best to calm our nerves. After all the tubes were set in place and the pain killers began to take hold, we waited for him to be admitted. Two hours later one of the nurses wheeled him to a room. After he was settled in, I gave him a kiss goodnight and drove home.

When I walked in the door Derek was standing in the kitchen waiting for me.

"What happened, Mom?"

"Dad fell off a deck at work."

"Why," he asked.

"Oh, because he felt like flying and breaking his ribs," I sarcastically replied.

"No, really. Why did he do this again?"

I thought of Derek's compassion for my sister and mother when their husbands died of cancer and wondered why he showed none of it for his father. So, I asked, "Why don't you get it? Dad didn't want this to happen. It was an accident. He didn't fall, break his ribs, and injure his lung on purpose. Think about it."

Derek raised his eyebrows, shook his head and said, "Sure," then went into is bedroom and turned on a videogame. Minutes later he came into the kitchen, tapped me on the back, and gave me a hug.

I believe that Charlie's accidents affected Derek personally and his reaction was that of fear. The loss of Danny and Chet was difficult to witness, but when his Dad was injured, he had no outlet other than anger. At best, it was the most logical conclusion I could conger up in my own mind.

Charlie was discharged from the hospital after a three day stay. He was in pretty bad shape physically and emotionally and blamed himself for the fall. The injuries sustained in the bike accident and the therapy needed to get back to work were ever present in his mind. However, this time was a bit different. His arm wasn't in a sling, so after the first follow-up, he was given permission to drive.

Derek continued to do well in the BOCES classes and came home more focused and excited about his afternoons. Because Charlie was home, he didn't need to call me at work after school and went directly into his room to play games. And, within a week of Charlie's recovery, the two of them were battling it out on some kind of dragon game until I got home. They went to action movies together and went gaga over Angelina Jolie in *Wanted.* In some way this time together was a blessing for both of them.

When it came time for Derek to go to the cardiologist, Charlie took him to Albany. This appointment was extremely important and I would have liked to go, too, but I had taken off too much time in February and we had a vacation planned in mid-August. Instead of taking the time off, I worried about it all day. When I got home after work, Derek was in his bedroom playing a video and Charlie was at the computer. "Charlie, what happened at the doctor's office?"

"They did the usual testing," he replied.

"And, did the doctor mention anything about his concerns?"

"No. It was weird. He said he wasn't sure why we were there."

"He's the one that told me he wanted to see Derek, he was worried about the test results. Did he say anything else," I asked.

"Yeah, he said that Derek should continue with his exercise and he'd write to Derek's general practitioner and suggest a cardiologist in our area because he was aging out of pediatric care."

So, it was. Charlie was recuperating and, for the exception of a small heart valve leak and a little *ABCDEFG*, Derek was well.

NO PLACE LIKE HOME

Though Derek had difficulty grasping social cues, he had no problem understanding how computers worked. He was excelling at BOCES and continued to pass his classes with flying colors. He found his niche and there was talk about him being able to get a job during the summer through Vocational Educational Services of Individuals with Disabilities, VESID. He'd be provided job training, resume' writing, and all he required to find a job in the computer repair field.

Charlie and I decided it was time to cut the apron strings and allow him to take a transit bus to Kingston on the weekend when he and Raymond decided to go to the movies or wanted to simply hang out at the mall. Saturday morning I sat with the guys and told them how things were going to work. I made sure they each had watches, ID cards, wallets, and enough money for the bus, the movie, lunch and an emergency. Then we checked the schedule to decide which bus they should take to get home.

I took them to the bus stop, waited for it to come, watched while they got on, and as the bus drove down the road. When it disappeared from sight I decided to check out a few yard sales. I headed toward Woodstock and saw *a huge four family yard sale*, which looked pretty bad from the road. I turned back toward the highway and saw another sign pointing east toward Kingston. There I found a pretty crystal vase for $5.00. Just before making a U-turn for home, I wondered whether the guys got to the mall on time. Oh what the hell, I thought, a trip into Kingston wouldn't kill me. I snuck around the back of the mall and waited until I saw Derek and Raymond get off the bus, then drove home.

As soon as I walked in the door I set my alarm clock, just in case I lost track of time while I sat at the computer. When the alarm rang, I felt as though someone was watching over me saying, "Stop being overly protective." I grabbed my purse, got in the car, and drove to the bus stop.

Because our rural bus system was a flag-down one, arrival times were approximate and notoriously late. After forty-five minutes I saw the bus in the distance and as it approached it showed no signs of stopping. I jumped out of the car and, as if the driver could hear me, yelled, "Stop the bus." Seconds later the bus stopped, the kids got out and walked to the car. Derek took one look at me, smacked his head, raised his eyebrows, and said, "Sorry Mom. We almost forgot." The bus trips became common place and, though I enjoyed my freedom, I missed my Saturdays with them.

As the school year came to an end we had a meeting with his VESID advisor. Unfortunately, I was either misinformed or I misunderstood the information given to me earlier in the year. Derek had hoped he would get a summer job in the computer world and was extremely disappointed when we learned he was ineligible. Apparently, someone forgot to tell us that VESID could only provide these services when he graduated twelfth grade.

He had no interest in going back to the grocery store or working anywhere close to home. He stopped at a couple stores in Kingston and filled out applications, but didn't get a call. I left a message with an acquaintance in local government and asked if there was a department in the county slated to help individuals with disabilities and, to my surprise, got a response the next day. One of the department heads agreed to work with Derek. Unfortunately, not only were the hours difficult, but there was no bus transportation to the site. I would have to get him there early in the morning and his day would end around 3:00 p.m. I called taxi cab companies, the county bus system, and friends who lived close to the area, but nothing worked. I called the department head and thanked him for his generous offer, but we had to decline. We just couldn't get Derek to the job site.

Just before the last week of school, Raymond arrived for his weekend stay. The guys went to the movies on Saturday, had a little fight about money and the arcade, and came back in less than happy moods. I spoke to them for a while and it seemed like the argument had been resolved.

That night, after Charlie and I returned from dinner with friends, we were sitting in the back room when I heard Derek scream at Raymond. "You take that back. Take it back now." I heard a loud bang, jumped up, opened the door, and saw Derek standing over Raymond with steam literally coming out of his ears.

I asked what the hell was going on and Derek said, "Raymond called me a fucking retard. He better take it back or else."

Apparently, the issues raised earlier in the day were not resolved and I had a long conversation with both of them. Things seemed to cool down that night, but Raymond left the next morning without saying goodbye. Derek was convinced he'd come back the following weekend, but he didn't. He called Raymond about fifteen times, but he never called back.

In the meantime, Kids Together, KT, was wrapping up for the year. Derek was *aging out* and wouldn't be able to return as a member of the group. As always, I attended the closing ceremony and, when it was time, I presented my award to Derek for maturity, a higher level of understanding, and his accomplishments at BOCES.

After all the parents handed out awards and the counselors handed out theirs. Derek's leader, Mark, called him to the center of the floor. He told everyone that Derek was the longest attendee of Kids Together and was considered the *captain* of the older group and that he shared so many stories and words of wisdom over the years that group wouldn't be the same without him. Derek's face lit up.

School was over, he didn't have a job, there was nothing set up through school, and he didn't have Raymond to occupy his time. We didn't want him sitting home every day playing videogames, eating too much and having nothing to do, so we spoke to the owner of a local animal rescue farm and decided that volunteer work would be worth a try. Derek wasn't thrilled with the idea, but I thought it might be a good experience.

It didn't take long before I knew he wasn't into working on a farm. He'd get up in the morning with a frown on his face, begrudgingly got in my car, and dragged his feet as he walked to the main house. He wasn't any happier when Charlie picked him up in the afternoon and we knew his days working at the farm were numbered. I wasn't surprised when I got a call from the owner telling me that Derek wasn't working out. She said he refused to work in the cows' pasture and kicked sand in a turkey's face, which was totally unacceptable. That night we spoke to Derek and he told us that he refused, under any circumstance, to pick up cow dung.

He called Raymond and left messages a couple times a week but never received a return call. He asked me to call Raymond's grandmother to see if there was something that could be done to bring his friend back, but I didn't. It was time for Derek to work harder at achieving friendships and, perhaps it was time to move on.

***

Kelly worked for a local community organization that helped teenagers find a place to belong. Derek had expressed an interest in learning how to skateboard and we thought he might be able to use that as a venue to develop new friendships. She met with us at home and started the intake process and, before she left that day, promised to look into a couple things for us while we were on vacation in Vermont. She hoped that she would be able to take him to the youth center in Woodstock to get him lessons, but it had to be cleared by her supervisor.

We decided that it was time for a camping trip. Charlie promised to take us to a nice hotel in Plattsburgh the first night of our journey before heading to Lake Champlain the following morning. I drove, Charlie navigated, and Derek sat in the back seat with the Mp3 plugged in his ear. We pointed out places of interest along the way and did our best to get Derek's attention, but he was intently listening to music and refused to be distracted.

At times I'd scream, "Derek, check out the water." No response.

Charlie yelled, "Derek, look at the boats." No response.

Once in a while, he'd see something along the way, take off his headphones, and say, "Hey, Mom, Dad, look at that."

After a long day on the road we finally reached Plattsburg and found our way to a Holiday Inn. They didn't have a single room available and suggested another hotel. The next one didn't have a vacancy either. The guy at the front desk told us that it would be difficult to find a room because of the state fair. Thankfully, he found a hotel with one room still available. We dashed to the car and with directions in hand made it to our destination within minutes. As we pulled into the parking lot I noticed another car was ahead of us. We parked behind them and watched as one of the passengers got out and ran toward the entrance. Unfortunately, they got the last room, but the reservation clerk said there was a motel within a twenty-mile radius that had a couple rooms left and he could reserve it for us if we wanted him to. We had no choice. He made the call, reserved the room, and gave us directions.

From a distance the place looked run down and, as we got closer, it looked even worse. I shot Charlie and evil glare and he knew he was in trouble for not reserving something ahead. But we were tired, it was getting late, and we had no place else to go. The driveway was pretty beat up, the pool was cracked and empty, and the grounds looked pretty bleak. However, the four beer-bellied rednecks partying behind their truck didn't seem to mind. The woman behind the front desk asked if we wanted to see the room so we got the key and took a look. In my estimation it was absolutely horrible. I checked for bugs in the bed, smelled the sheets, and checked the bathroom. Even though the place looked and felt absolutely disgusting, on the surface, it seemed pretty clean. Charlie and Derek were upset about the situation but I was downright angry. As soon as our things were in the room we left to get the ferry schedule to Lake Champlain and to find a nice place to eat.

Unfortunately, the rest of the town was pretty run down and the only restaurant available was the one at our lovely motel. So there we were, sitting in a sticky booth looking at yellowed copies of the menu. Charlie and Derek placed their orders and I stopped gritting my teeth long enough to give the waitress mine. While we waited for our food, Derek took off to the game room to watch a guy playing pool. The man acknowledged him, showed him a couple moves, and before we knew it Derek was sinking balls. He was pretty proud of himself and had a smile on his face throughout dinner. The food was surprisingly good and the tension in my head and body released before we went to bed.

The next morning we got up early enough to catch the first ferry and when we got to Grand Isle State Park there were plenty of camping and lean-to sites available. We had camped in lean-tos before and, as far as we were concerned, there wasn't a downside. They were open air, the tent could stay wrapped on the car rack, and we could watch the stars from bed at night. After we chose our site we unpacked our gear, changed our clothes, and headed toward the interpretive center. There were some kids hanging around and, to my surprise, Derek took charge and said hello. They responded in kind and I hoped he would continue a conversation but, instead, he walked out and walked to the beach. Charlie and I followed him and the three of us sat at the water's edge and looked at the view until it started to drizzle.

That night the weather cleared and Charlie made a fire and cooked burgers on the grill for dinner. Not long after we sat to eat we had a visitor from the neighborhood. A well fed cat decided to stay for scraps and a bit of petting around the ears. Having had his fill, our furry friend decided to move on to the next campsite.

With a roaring fire in the backdrop, we played a game of Scrabble and then got ready for bed. The three of us talked about the day and reminisced about the horrible motel we were at the night before.

Not long after I closed my eyes I heard an animal approach the site.

"Hey, guys. Do you hear something," I whispered.

"Yea, maybe it's a raccoon," Derek replied.

Charlie shuffled around near his sleeping bag and found his flashlight. It wasn't a raccoon and it wasn't a bear, it was our furry friend sitting in our lean-to. In the middle of the night Derek whispered to me "Mom, the cat is sleeping with me. I'm rubbing its back, it's purring and it's not afraid of me." The next morning Derek was asleep with the cat at his side. It hung around until after breakfast and then took off into the woods.

While Charlie set off on a bike ride along Lake Champlain, Derek and I went in search of a grocery store and a someplace to swim. We found a sandy beach about fifteen minutes south of the campsite and I promised we'd go back after Charlie returned from his ride and we finished lunch. It was a cool, damp, un-beach like day, but we didn't have anything else planned.

For a mid-August day, it felt more like October and very few people were brave enough to swim. Charlie and I told Derek that it was too cold for us to go in the water, but he could care less about the weather or the temperature. He jumped in and begged the two of us to join him. Thankfully, just before I started to cave in, it started to rain.

On our way back to the campsite the clouds began to give way to the sun and no more than two minutes after we got out of the car, Derek grabbed our towels and asked us to follow him down the path to the swimming area. There were quite a few campers excited about the break in the weather and the grassy knoll above the lake's shore was lined with beach chairs and blankets.

After jumping in for a quick swim, Charlie and I went back to our place on the knoll and Derek stayed in long enough to find a friend to swim with. It ended up being a warm, lazy, enjoyable summer afternoon.

The next morning we packed up and headed for Smuggler's Notch and Stowe. Charlie had been there with his friend Kemp a couple years before and he wanted us to experience the area. He pointed out beautiful scenery along the way and, every once in a while, we'd attempt to get Derek's attention.

"Derek, take that stupid Mp3 out of your ear. We're trying to talk to you," Charlie yelled.

He shot back, "Why don't you shut up?"

"Take them out now," I demanded.

The last thing I needed was a screaming match during the entire vacation so I had to come up with a plan.

"Look kiddo, would you take that thing out of your ear if I signal *time* out?"

He begrudgingly agreed.

A little while later Charlie mentioned that the waterslide Derek wanted to go to was coming up so I tried to get his attention.

He grunted and said, "That's the wrong signal. You did it wrong. Your fingers are too far apart."

Whatever I yelled, "Dad just wanted you to see the waterslide we just passed!"

"Oh, sorry," he whispered.

A little while later we were in Stowe searching out a place to stay for a night or two. Not far from town we found a very nice hotel with a pool, a pond for fishing, and a very nice restaurant. After checking in and unpacking the car we walked around the property and discussed our plans during our stay. Derek had his heart set on the waterslide,

Charlie wanted to take a bike ride up the notch and back, and I wanted to go into town to check out the shops.

Even though the weather was iffy, Charlie and I decided to take Derek to the waterslide to get it over with. They grabbed their suits and a couple of towels and as we made our way up the mountain, a large rain cloud loomed overhead. A few drops of rain hit the windshield along the way, but we were committed to the adventure, rain or shine. As soon as Charlie parked the car, Derek grabbed their stuff and walked as quickly as possible toward the lodge.

Derek was psyched. He had waited for this moment for days and, after watching some people slide down the mountain, he high-tailed it to the ticket counter. Of course, as soon as he got there, it was announced that the waterslide was closed due to rain.

Charlie suggested we check out a gondola ride up the road and we promised Derek to come back if it stopped raining. Unfortunately, the rain didn't let up the entire time we were on the ride and it didn't look as if it was going to stop.

When we pulled out of the parking lot and made the turn down the road, Derek asked, "Mom, where's my Mp3?"

"I don't know. Charlie, did you see his Mp3?"

"Nope, I don't have it," Charlie replied.

Derek screamed, "You took it. Where is it?"

"We didn't take it. I have no idea where it is," I replied.

"Give it back to me, Mom!"

"I didn't take your damn Mp3."

Sure, the thing drove us crazy, but we wouldn't get rid of it. Charlie and I looked around the front of the car and neither of us found it. I told Derek to keep looking in the back seat but he got so angry I had Charlie pull over to the side of the road. I got out of the car, opened Derek's door, and demanded he get out.

"If you think we have it Derek, check my pockets. Here's my purse. Look in the glove box and find it," I yelled.

He shot me the evil eye and cursed under his breath while he checked the interior of the car and, at some point, realized we weren't the culprits.

He apologized for accusing us and after we both calmed down, we retraced the last couple hours. He had it in the lodge by the waterslide but he didn't bring it on the gondola. Perhaps, he left it in the lodge when he stopped to buy a drink.

Charlie drove us back to the ski area and I told Derek to go to the cafeteria and check with the person at the register. We sat in the car when he went in, shook our heads in total frustration, and waited for him to return. From a distance I could see him walking back with something in his hand and a smile on his face. Thanks to an honest kid, he got his Mp3 back.

Looking back it was the worst part of the vacation but it had a lasting effect. From that point forward his attitude and behavior changed. It was as though something clicked in his head. He walked lighter on his feet, was less abrupt, and had a calmer demeanor.

Later that day, Charlie took us to a restaurant for lunch and Derek had his first non-alcoholic beer. We sat at our table having significant conversation and, when we left to walk to the car, Derek put his arm around me and gave me a kiss on my forehead. He thanked Charlie as we drove back to the hotel and we each sighed in relief.

The next day, while Charlie went on a cycling ride up the 20 mile stretch of roadway known as the *notch*, Derek and I went into town to check out the shops and look for information about a waterslide park near Bromley. With a brochure in hand, we went back to the hotel, packed up the car, and waited for Charlie by the pool. Because of the twisty, tight, hairpin turns of Smuggler's Notch, I was relieved to see him peddle into the parking lot a little after noon.

After taking a quick dip in the pool, he loaded the bike on the back of the car and we headed down the road. Charlie had his heart set on gold panning near Plymouth, Vermont.

Coolidge State Park had an entire loop of lean-to campsites with sweeping views of the Green Mountains and we were lucky enough to get a beautiful site. The park was within a short driving distance of Echo Lake, Plymouth State Park, and recreational gold panning on Buffalo Brook.

Derek and I spent the next two days swimming at the lake while Charlie panned nearby. At night, we sat near the campfire, roasted marshmallows, played board games, and laughed a lot. We had a good time and I felt a bit sad to leave, but it was time for the last leg of our trip.

The Bromley Waterslide Park looked pretty exciting and, considering our day at Stowe and Derek's amazing turnaround, we decided to spend a big part of our day there. However, when we arrived it was blatantly obvious that the brochure was designed to lure customers to a less than thrilling park. Charlie and Derek found one slide they enjoyed, but after walking up the hill and sliding down about ten times, they were done.

After lunch we left for our friends' house. Judy and Dave had recently built a second home on a private lake near Oneonta and we loved it there. The guys were planning to hang out on the dock where Derek caught his first fish the year before and I planned on spending time with Judy swimming, sitting in the sun, going for a walks, and simply relaxing.

The drive took a lot longer than we thought it would, but we made it there by early afternoon. It was great to see the two of them and, after spending the last few days camping, the luxury of a house was more than appealing. We spent time on the dock and relaxed by the lake in the afternoon. Dave cooked on the grill in the early evening and we all went for a walk, picked berries, and enjoyed our time together.

When we got back to the house Charlie, Dave, Judy, and I sat on the deck sipping wine and conversing while Derek watched a movie. By 10:00 p.m. we were all a little tired and decided to call it a day.

Our room had a full sized bed and a couch that opened up, so Charlie and I got the bed and Derek got the couch. Charlie and Derek fell asleep pretty quickly. But, as usual, I was restless and had a difficult time falling asleep. After about an hour of starring at the ceiling I heard Derek toss and turn. Then he began to make an odd grunting sound as if he was having a nightmare.

"Derek, wake up." There was no response. I spoke a little louder, "Derek, wake up." Again, no response. The grunting seemed to get more intense and a little scary. I got out of bed, walked over to him and rubbed his back. "Derek, honey, wake up."

He didn't move. I touched the back of his legs, got a little closer to him, and felt his whole body shaking.

"Derek, wake up," I shouted. My heart sunk.

I yelled out, "Charlie, come here. Something's wrong with Derek."

"He won't wake up, something is wrong." Charlie shook him and nothing happened. He yelled out and there was no response. We turned him around and I opened his eyelid. He was non-responsive. I ran down to Judy and Dave's room and woke them.

"Judy, Dave, we have to get an ambulance. Something's wrong with Derek." They jumped up, a little dazed, and I explained what was happening. Judy stayed with Charlie and I hopped into Dave's car. We had to find the quickest place to get phone service and, as Dave sped up the road to the top of the hill, I was able to dial 911. Dave took the phone from me to give directions to the house, while I shook in fright. The paramedics were on the way.

When we got back to the house I ran to the door and began climbing the stairs when I heard Judy and Charlie yell, "Pat, he's awake. He's awake." I ran to his bed and saw a completely dazed, confused and weakened Derek. Charlie said that it seemed like he had a stroke.

Judy said she rubbed his back while the two of them tried to wake Derek up and when he gained consciousness he seemed to have trouble moving. The paramedics arrived and I watched as they examined him. He seemed a little better with time, but there was something horribly wrong. More responders showed up at the house and after their examination they decided that more than likely it was a seizure. Derek spoke with the paramedics and they decided that he could walk down the stairs rather than being carried to the ambulance.

Charlie and I drove to the hospital behind them, with Judy and Dave not far behind. My mind was racing and my body shook as I watched the ambulance pull into the emergency entrance. Charlie quickly found a parking spot and we rushed into the hospital as they wheeled Derek in. The EMT told us to go to the medical clerk's counter to give his medical history and insurance information. We sat for what seemed like an eternity, giving her Derek's date of birth, residence, etc., before we were directed to his side. He was lethargic, confused, and couldn't remember a thing—not a dream, not our screaming, not the shaking, nothing.

I rubbed his head and Charlie held his leg as we waited for the doctor. It took an inordinate amount of time for him to arrive and, when he nonchalantly waltzed into the room, I was upset. We explained that Derek had a mild heart valve leak and PDD. The doctor looked at me with a quizzical stare. It was obvious he had no idea what PDD was, so I told him that our guy's diagnosis was on the autistic spectrum and that he typically had a speech delay.

Derek was still groggy and his speech was understandably slower than usual. Even though he was awake, it was apparent that he was not himself. Charlie and I were extremely concerned, but the doctor didn't seem to be. He shared the paramedic's diagnosis of an onset, sleep deprived seizure. His blood pressure was a little high but he said that very often happens with seizures. I repeated that he had a minor heart valve leak, but according to the doctor, it wasn't a contributing factor.

As they wheeled Derek in for a CAT scan we went out to the waiting room and met with Dave and Judy, told them that Derek would be okay and that they should go home. Charlie and I went back in the room to wait for Derek to return from testing. We held each other for a minute and cried.

When they finally rolled him through the door he seemed to be a bit more aware of his surroundings. He asked why he was in the hospital and we explained that he might have had a seizure. However, when they returned with the results, the doctor said that the CAT scan was inconclusive and that it was almost impossible to detect a seizure unless it happens at the time of the test. Our options were to have him stay in the hospital for observation without the benefit of a specialist, or to go home and make an appointment with a local neurologist. We discussed our choices with Derek and the three of us decided it was time to go home. Charlie pulled the car up to the entrance, I helped him get in and, with the exception of a few cautiously optimistic words, I sat silently in shock until we got back to Judy and Dave's.

We thanked them for their hospitality, their concern, and friendship, packed up, and said our goodbyes. Charlie drove home while I sat with my teeth clenched and held in my tears. Half way home my legs began to shake uncontrollably. Enough was enough. Derek was doing so much better and his life was improving. Now what? He slept most of the way home.

When we pulled in the driveway both Charlie and I told Derek that we wanted him to rest on the couch during the day so we could keep an eye on him. I put blankets on the couch and he stayed there watching TV, nodding out every once in a while. By dinner time he seemed a bit better, had a healthy meal, and began acting a bit more like himself. I insisted we both sleep in the living room on our L-shaped couch and he didn't argue. He slept while I maintained watch over him. Every once in a while I checked his head, his heart beat, and asked if he was okay. He had no event during the night and seemed fine in the morning. I was exhausted.

BURSTS OF LIGHT

Sunday morning we told Derek we wanted him to take it easy and discouraged him from sitting in front of the TV and playing video games.

After breakfast we took a ride to Jessica and Ed's house to tell them about our vacation and his incident and, even though he seemed a bit better, he was visibly concerned. He sat on the couch and tried to explain to everyone what happened, but shrugged his shoulders when asked what a seizure felt like. All he knew was that it made him a little tired and a little worried.

Trudy willingly agreed to let him stay with her the next day so that we could maintain a twenty-four-hour watch until he was seen by his doctor. I called the neurologist's office to get an appointment as soon as possible, but the receptionist was less than cooperative. I tried to explain how important it was for Derek to be seen and that we could be there at any time, of any day, to see any doctor. Finally, she gave me a date about a week and a half out, but he needed a referral.

I called his general practitioner and we got an appointment for the next day, but I had to get the ER notes from the hospital. I called the hospital and they agreed to fax them over.

I must have had concern written all over my face when we walked into the office because the nurse didn't give us a chance to sit in the waiting area. She brought us right into an examination room where we were met by the doctor.

Derek's blood pressure was a little elevated but he wasn't too concerned. After examining him and questioning me about the event, he concurred with the emergency room doctor. He said, "Kids like Derek have been known to have seizures, but that everything would be fine." While we waited for the nurse to bring us the referral, he told me that it wouldn't hurt to maintain a watch until we saw the neurologist. Then, before saying goodbye, he told Derek that he was a great kid and that he was lucky to have me as a mom.

After that visit I felt a little more comfortable allowing him to sleep in his bed, but I checked in on him every hour, touching his head slightly and putting my hand on his back to be sure he was breathing.

I called his caseworker, Kelly, to tell her what happened and suggested we hold off on the skateboarding lessons until we saw the neurologist. She was saddened that Derek was having problems and agreed to visit with him during the week, complete her intake, and figure out what she could do for him in the meantime. She said that her director wasn't thrilled about the skateboarding lessons and thought she might take him to the youth center in Woodstock until they figured something else out.

I didn't get much sleep while maintaining a watch over our guy and couldn't wait to go to the neurologist to get some answers. The afternoon of the appointment I made sure we got there early enough to fill out the necessary forms before being called in. The receptionist handed me a clipboard with the typical paper work and questionnaire to fill out. I had completed so many of these forms in the past that I was able to get it back to her quickly. We waited for at least a half hour before getting anxious. I asked the receptionist how long it would take before we saw the doctor and was told *a little while.* An hour later we were still waiting. I told Derek I had a feeling they were all going to turn the lights off, shut down the office, and leave us there. We laughed, but it wasn't funny. Finally, a nurse called his name and we were led to the doctor's office.

The neurologist asked Derek what happened and I explained that he didn't remember a thing. I went through the entire night's events, told him what happened at the hospital, and how Derek reacted afterward. He, too, thought it was a sleep deprived seizure and stated that "kids like this" were known to develop them.

Derek asked him, "How can you swallow your tongue?"

The doctor laughed and told him, "People don't swallow their tongues. Sometimes when a person has a seizure they bite a piece of it off and choke."

"Well that's a relief," Derek replied.

The doctor told us that people don't die from seizures and that Derek would be *fine.*

We talked about skateboarding and our plan for a fun filled day at a water park with Jessica and the kids and he told us that we could do anything we felt comfortable with and, yes, skateboarding and a waterslide park would be okay.

The next step was an MRI and an EEG. The MRI was scheduled for the following week, but the EEG with EKG trace would have to wait until the technicians were fully staffed after summer vacations. I wasn't thrilled and asked the doctor if he could schedule it sooner. He said he'd see what he could do, but when I spoke to the scheduling nurse she said we'd have to wait a month. I begged her to ask the doctor to speed it up and she went back to his office to speak to him, but when she returned she said he didn't think it was urgent enough. So, the MRI was scheduled for the following Wednesday and the EEG was scheduled for September 24th. I was upset about having to wait so long for the second test, but the thought of life going on without modifications was encouraging.

The next day I called Kelly and told her that Derek had no medical restrictions and asked that she try to find something to boost his ego. In the meantime, I promised to find a place to get him skateboard lessons and told Jessica we could go to a waterslide park.

That Saturday we packed up the car and headed up north to Zoom Flume and, with the exception of me falling on the pavement and scraping my knees and Nicole getting a splinter in her foot, the day was fantastic. The kids had a blast. They spent all day together running from one waterslide to the other while I rode the lazy river. At the end of the day we promised each other that we'd return the following year.

Unlike MRI's in the past, this one went quickly. There were no worries about Derek's ability to lie still in the tube. He had a few of them over the last couple years and wasn't bothered by the noise.

The next day I got a call from Kelly. "Pat, I found something for Derek and I think you'll be thrilled. I spoke to a guy named Bob who lives in your school district and works with kids like Derek. He's a mentor who engages kids in exercise, will help him with his school work, encourage him to get his driver's license, and help him develop a positive attitude"

"Fantastic. Can you set up a meeting with him as soon as possible?"

"Sure, I'll get a hold of him and call you right back."

The meeting was scheduled for 5:00 p.m. the following day and Kelly agreed to pick Derek up at home so I could leave work on time and meet them at the Bob's house.

When we arrived we were greeted by a highly motivated gentleman with an extremely positive attitude. Derek seemed a little overwhelmed and, instead of perking up, was more quiet than usual. We discussed Derek's difficulty making friends and how important it was to empower him. We talked about his lack of exercise, the minor heart valve leak, and the fact that he most likely experienced an onset sleep deprived seizure.

Bob explained that his brother had suffered from seizures and, because Derek's neurologist did not restrict him and the cardiologist wanted him to exercise, we decided to go ahead with a plan. By the time the meeting was over it was agreed that he'd develop an exercise regimen, work with Derek to complete his homework, and help him get his license. Derek listened to the plan and was less than enthusiastic, but when he heard he might be able to work with swords, his eyes lit up and he was ready to start.

In the meantime, I searched the internet for skateboard lessons and spoke to Matt, an instructor who worked at a skating rink in Accord. First, I told him about Derek's balance issues, but explained that he was quite an accomplished skier. I told him about the seizure and that the neurologist wasn't restricting his activity. Then, I told him I was desperate to find someone who'd be willing to work with him and, to my surprise, he was willing to give it a try. His first lesson was scheduled during the weekend.

That Saturday we took the long drive to the skating rink where we met Matt.

It was obvious that he listened to everything I told him during our telephone conversation and he knew exactly how to handle Derek. I gave them the space they needed to work together, grabbed a magazine, and sat by the tables out of sight. Every once in a while I'd listen to them and, for very short periods of time, I heard the skateboard roll.

There were thumps in between with a few grunts during the lesson, but Derek was determined. When the hour was up, Matt told me that he did very well considering his balance issues and told Derek that he should be proud of himself. The next lesson was scheduled for the Saturday after Labor Day.

We had nothing planned for the holiday, so Charlie and I decided to have one of our fabulous yard sales. He set up old tools and a myriad of old, rusty things he had in his shop. I went through the house and found old toys, games, clothes, glassware, crystal and a variety of things we had been holding onto for a while. Charlie ran around putting the signs up and Derek set up tables while I brought my loot outside.

After the signs were up people started to stop at the house. Men, women and children stopped to look at Charlie's stuff and bought old rusty tools, but when they looked at Derek's and my things they walked away. On Saturday Charlie sold quite a bit and I sold my typical $10.00 to $20.00 worth of garbage. I really hate yard sales.

Derek wanted to go to Kingston and, without Raymond around, the only one he could nag was me. On Sunday morning I told him if he stayed outside with me, sold some of his stuff, and received enough money to buy the new gaming system he craved, I'd take him in that afternoon.

Once again we took out tables, chairs, and the things that couldn't be left outside at night. People started to stop by and spent their time at Charlie's table but no one wanted any of Derek's or my junk.

By lunch time he started to obsess about the new PlayStation and begged me to take him to Kingston and purchase it for him. Money was tight and he spent all of fifteen minutes helping me with the yard sale. I was in no mood to accommodate him.

He got so angry he slammed his bedroom door, started to scream, and I replied by turning the stereo on loud enough to drown him out.

He ran out of his bedroom, turned off the music, yelled at me for ignoring him, ran back to his room, and slammed the door again. In the heat of the argument, my emotions ran high, and I reduced myself to an angry child. I turned the music up again. He stomped out of his room and a screaming match between the two of us got out of hand. After he raised his hand at me and I knocked it down, he ran back toward his room and screamed, "You hate me. You wish I was dead. I'm a fucking idiot."

I retreated outside to my tables and waited about five minutes before going back into the house and knocking on his door. "Can I come in Derek? I need to talk to you." No answer. "Derek, come in my bedroom. We need to talk." He came out, gave me the evil eye, followed me into my room, plopped down on the bed and said, "What?"

"Derek, I don't hate you."

He took a deep breath and sighed.

I put my arms around him and told him that one of the best days in my life was the day he was born. Sure, at times, things were tough. But I loved him deeply and the last thing I wanted was for him to die.

"Look, kiddo. When we have a fight you run to your bedroom, slam the door, and scream until your throat hurts. I can't do that."

We had a long talk and by the end of it I felt we had resolved some issues. We gave each other a hug and I thought the matter was settled. I went back outside and he sat at the computer.

A few minutes later he handed me a piece of paper and ran back into the house. The note read:

"Hey mom, I'm sorry that I started this whole darned fight and I hope we can make up and try not to do this again. If we do this again then we will hate one another... but let us just forgive each other and forget this whole fight ... ok once again, I'm sorry 4 the fight. From: Derek"

I followed him back into the house to thank him and found him crying in his bedroom closet with a lit candle and an egg timer. I asked him to come out, but he motioned that he wasn't ready. I waited in the living room for what felt like an awfully long time, then went back in and asked him to come out. He still wasn't ready.

I brought him a soda named "Calm," placed it on the floor, walked away, and waited. A little while later he came out, we held each other for a while, then went outside to pack up our crap. It was a moment that still weighs heavily in my heart.

The next day I talked him into going swimming in the pool with me. After all, it would be closed up soon and it was a beautiful warm, sunny day. We were both feeling angst from the day before and it seemed like the perfect time to let it go.

As usual, Derek jumped right in, but it took a while for me to succumb to the cold water. When I finally gave in, he asked me to float. I leaned back toward the water and he gently placed his hands behind my back. I looked up and saw my handsome young man with a hint of whiskers on his otherwise smooth face and spiked blonde hair. With his tanned torso gliding me swiftly through the water, I gently floated to the current of the whirlpool created by our movement. I took a breath and gazed at the sky. It was the sharpest color blue with soft, slowly moving, wispy clouds. As the whirlpool slowed down he let go and dove deep within the pool. When I stood up he grabbed my legs, lifted me as high as is possible, let out a huge laugh, and dunked me. I swam to the surface coughing up water, moved my hair from my eyes, and took a deep breath. He moved close to me, gently putting his hands on my shoulder, then leaned closer and planted a wet, sweet, soft, kiss on my lips. "Sorry, Mom."

***

The first day of school I got a call at work. Apparently he missed the BOCES bus and they needed to know what to do. Our house was less than a mile away and I was forty minutes from school. As far as I was concerned, he could walk home.

I called Charlie to tell him what happened and he decided to see if he could catch up with him on his way home for lunch. That night he told me that when he caught up with Derek he was breathing hard, his face was red, and he was sweating a lot. We were worried about his heart and hoped that Bob would convince him to exercise and help him lose some weight.

***

That Friday, before leaving work, I got a call from Charlie. "Pat, you won't believe who's here. Raymond showed up. He had the bus driver drop him off at the school. He's staying for the weekend."

Derek was thrilled to have his buddy back and Charlie and I were relieved. They hung out in the bedroom, played videogames, and spent time outside with the swords they made in Charlie's shop months before.

Derek had his skateboarding lesson on Saturday morning and, for the most part, the guys hung out in the afternoon without any mention of the argument they had months before. But Derek, apparently, was getting on Raymond's nerves because he came into the kitchen around dinner time and asked me, "How do you deal with him 24/7?"

"I don't know, Raymond. I just think there's a reason. Why do you keep coming back," I asked.

"Because Derek needs me and I need to be here," he replied.

That night I made a really nice meal in celebration of Raymond's return. The guys spent the better part of the evening playing videogames and went to bed around 11:00 p.m.

Sunday morning after breakfast, I called Raymond's house to find out when someone was picking him up. His dad said that they didn't' have a clue that Raymond was spending the weekend with us. In fact, he didn't have their permission. At that moment I knew it wasn't Raymond's choice to stay away for the summer. He took advantage of the school's transportation the first chance he got and it reconciled their friendship. Raymond's father picked him up early that afternoon and Derek got ready for his first workout with Bob.

OUR WARRIOR

Just before 4:00 that afternoon we hopped in the car and headed to Bob's house. When we arrived, he met us in the driveway. The man emanated positivity and seemed extremely eager for the challenge.

"Pat, we'll be done in an hour."

"Come on handsome, let's get to work"

He motioned to Derek to follow him and they headed for the backyard. While they worked together I took the time to look for the last blackberries of the season and checked my watch from time to time. Just before 5:00 I drove back to Bob's house. Derek worked hard and Bob was very happy with his performance. We agreed that he'd have his second lesson after school on Wednesday.

Derek took the bus to the beginning of Bob's street, walked down to the house, and made it in time for his session. Charlie picked him up afterwards and that night he told us about the exercises he did and mentioned that his stomach seemed to be getting a little tighter. He was proud of himself and looked forward to the next session, but a visit from Raymond on Friday and his skateboarding lesson on Saturday were on top of his agenda.

When I got home from work on Friday I expected to see Raymond. Derek told me he was sick again and wouldn't be able to come over. We knew better.

The next morning we went to Accord for his skateboarding lesson. He worked extremely hard and Matt told him that he'd be rolling on his own the following weekend. Derek was a skateboarder and there was no doubt that he was extremely proud of himself. The smile on his face couldn't be wider. It took a lot of energy to balance and maintain concentration and the sweat on his brow and redness in his face indicated how difficult it was. But, he was skateboarding.

I stopped at the closest convenience store to buy gas and a drink for Derek. After I pumped the gas and met Derek in the store, I saw that he not only had a large iced tea but a big bottle of soda as well. I told him I wasn't paying for both drinks and he got upset with me.

"Mom, I'm really thirsty. It's really hot out. I just worked really hard." I wasn't buying both drinks. "Derek, pick one and meet me in the car. I'll get you something else to drink when we get to Olive Day."

Olive Day was an annual event that included a penny social, food, music, yard sale items, craft booths, frog jumping contests, EMT's giving free blood pressure tests, political booths, and roaming politicians. Derek and I had gone to the event every year since he was little. We'd meet lots of friends from town and Jessica and Ed were bringing the kids.

As usual, our first stop was the penny social. I bought about $10 worth of tickets and Derek and I put them in the cans next to our favorite items. We walked around together for a bit, then I went my way and he went his. I met with our friend Bill, Derek's ski instructor, and I told him how proud I was of Derek's accomplishments; that he was doing so well at BOCES, skiing wonderfully, learning to skateboard, and working with a mentor. Bill had seen a lot of positive changes and I was thrilled to know that there were people within the community who appreciated our challenge.

A little while later I was talking to my friend Deb, from the theater, when Derek came by to tell me that he was really hot and feeling little dizzy. It was an extremely hot day and everyone was feeling it. I told him to get something cold to drink, sit at a picnic table in the pavilion, and to take it easy. After Deb and I finished our conversation, I went to the pavilion to check on him. I passed people dancing in front of the band and found Derek sitting next to Christina, his fifth grade teacher's assistant. He seemed a little cooler and was extremely happy to have found his old friend. Jessica and the kids were there, too. We stayed there until the music stopped and the winning penny social tickets were called. I won a one hour message therapy session and, while I waited for the gift certificate, Derek mentioned that he was still feeling a little weird. It was time to head home.

He seemed better during our ride home. We took a quick dip in the pool and by dinner time he seemed fine.

Charlie and I had planned to go to dinner with friends that night to celebrate my birthday and our friend Adrianne's. I checked with Derek several times to be sure he was feeling better and, once I was convinced he'd be okay, I promised to be home as soon as possible. We had a great time at dinner and when we returned home Derek surprised us with a treat he had baked while we were gone.

Charlie went to bed after eating his treat and Derek and I stayed up to watch TV. It was one of those memorable kind of nights with him on one side of our L-shaped couch and me on the other. My big guy looked at me and pouted just as he did when he was a toddler.

"Mom, would you rub my head?"

"Awe, come on Derek, I'm tired."

"Please," he asked.

"Okay kiddo, come over here, I'll rub your head for a while, as long as you rub my back when I'm finished."

He moved over, put his head in my lap, and I rubbed it until we were just about ready to fall asleep. When it was my turn, I laid on my stomach, he sat beside me and gently rubbed by back.

The next morning we got up and went through our normal Sunday morning routine. Charlie went to the store for the paper while I made the traditional bacon and eggs.

Charlie planned a bike ride during the afternoon and I decided to hang out at home and finish some chores before taking Derek to Bob's.

After breakfast I cleaned up around the kitchen, Charlie went outside to do yard work, and Derek was back in his room playing video games.

An hour or so later Charlie left for his bike ride and I knocked on Derek's door. "Do you want to go in the pool?"

"Not really."

"Are you sure? It might be the last time this summer."

"That's okay," he replied.

"Want to go for a walk?"

"No. Can we go to Al's and get something there?"

"All right, maybe I'll find a good cheese squash and we'll make a pie next week"

He shut the game down, bolted out of his room, and followed me while I searched for my shoes. He sat on the bed next to me as I slipped my shoes on, then walked one step behind me. As we left the bedroom he reached from behind me, put his arms around my waist and clasped his hands at my stomach. I stopped and tried to pull away but he had a pretty good hold. Then, he gave me a quick squeeze and held tight. I tried to unclasp his hands but he was too strong.

"Come on Derek, cut it out. You're driving me crazy. Do you want to go to Al's or not?"

He let me go, kissed the back of my head and laughed aloud. Then he grabbed the car keys, jumped in the passenger seat, and turned the car on while I searched for my purse.

While at the farm stand I found the perfect squash and Derek picked a few items.

As we stood in line he tried to persuade me to buy more than I was willing.

"Mom, I'm really thirsty. Can I get two juices?"

"Derek, I'm buying one. Put the other one back."

"Fine. So, I'll die of thirst."

"Derek, just put it back."

Sundays always flew by and this one was no exception. Before I knew it, it was time to take Derek to Bob's.

"Mom, it's time to go."

"Oh god, Derek. Wait a minute. I have to write a check and a quick note."

I rushed to find my checkbook and a piece of note paper, wrote quickly, grabbed my keys, and we were off.

When we got there I noticed other cars in the driveway. Bob was running a little late. As we stood waiting, I put my arms around my guy.

"Derek, I'm so glad that you decided to go ahead with this training. I'm so proud of you. You know, if you work really hard at this your life will change for the better."

"Yeah, I know Mom."

Within a few minutes Bob came out to greet us. He explained to Derek that they'd be working on exercise and might have time to work with the swords. Derek's eyes lit up. He was extremely excited.

I turned toward him. We stood face to face. I looked up, then placed my hand on his chest.

"Do a good job kiddo, have fun and I'll see you around 5:00. I'm going over to Annette and Greg's for a while."

During my visit we sat on the porch sipping wine and expressing relief that our kids were doing well. Derek finally found his niche in school. He was determined to get in shape, earn his driver's license, and turn his life around. For a change I saw a brighter future. Annette and Greg were cautiously optimistic that their son would survive his first week of college.

I was so relaxed sitting with my friends that late September afternoon I didn't want to leave. After all, Bob was running late and he'd hang out with Derek for a little while.

Five minutes after saying goodbye to my friends I pulled into Bob's driveway. There was a mother and her son outside waiting for Derek's session to end. I told them he was running late and was sure they wouldn't have to wait too long.

As we waited, I heard noises coming from the house and imagined Derek working hard with Bob's enthusiastic encouragement.

The young man waiting asked his mother if he could go inside to see what was going on. She agreed and he ran into the house. Within seconds he bolted through the door and asked me, "Are you Derek's mother? He needs you inside right away." I ran in and found them in the back room. Derek was on the floor and Bob was leaning over him giving him CPR. Derek's face was blue.

I yelled, "What happened?"

I could hear an ambulance in the background and Bob yelled at me, "Pat, grab the phone, they need to talk to you. One of the EMT's began giving me CPR instructions as I screamed them out.

It seemed like an eternity before they arrived.

As soon as the EMT's took over, Bob grabbed me and brought me to the kitchen.

I screamed, "He's dying, he's dying. What happened?"

"I thought he had a seizure but he didn't. I tossed a hacky-sack to him, he reached down then dropped to the floor."

Bob held me tightly as I screamed. I could feel my entire body shake, my feet stomping on the floor. Bob said, "Call Derek back, call him back." I screamed, "Derek, come back. Please don't die."

A state trooper appeared in the room. He told Bob he needed to talk to him and told me the EMTS were working on Derek and that they were bringing him to the hospital.

I grabbed the phone, ran outside, and called Charlie.

"Charlie, you have to come here right away. Something is wrong. I think Derek is dying. Come here."

It was as though time stood still. I paced frantically back and forth screaming, "Oh god, oh god, don't take my boy. Don't die, don't die."

Charlie got there just as they were lifting Derek into the ambulance. He walked into chaos. I was absolutely hysterical. He reached for me and we held on tight and cried.

The policeman gave Charlie a quick overview of the situation and said that he'd follow the ambulance and take us to the hospital. We got in the back of the van and Charlie and I held each other tightly as I trembled. While I tried to explain what I saw, the trooper asked us, "How old was your son?" I replied, with voice quivering, tears streaming down my cheeks to my lips, "He's not a *was* because he's not dead." The trooper picked up speed.

At the hospital we were directed to sit in the emergency room waiting area. Within a few minutes an emergency room doctor came in to talk to us. She said, "It doesn't look good."

I screamed, "No, he can't be dead. No!" She said she was sorry and told us she had to go back in.

I told Charlie I had to call Jessica and started to look for the pay phone. A man in the waiting room handed me his cell phone and I called. "Jessica, we're at Benedictine. I think Derek is dying."

She yelled, "I'll be there. I'm leaving now. I love you." I handed the phone back, sat down with Charlie and we continued crying hysterically. Within a few minutes a nurse asked us to follow her into the emergency room. We sat in a small room and waited for the doctor. When she walked in, I knew.

She said, "I'm so sorry. He's gone."

EPILOGUE

Over the years I've wondered why I felt it necessary to tell my story to the world. I did nothing spectacular—I loved my child. I don't have all the answers and quite frankly, at times, feel I have absolutely nothing to offer. But, as I got closer to this chapter in my life I understood why my story is so important.

Derek was given to us as a gift and we were blessed to have him in our lives for as long as he was. He gave me the opportunity to learn about so many wonderful children who suffer similar difficulties. I've developed so much respect for the counselors who do their best to preserve the well-being of us all and, for that, I truly thank them.

I knew Derek more than anyone else on this earth. I spent more time fighting with him and for him, and loved him more deeply than perhaps I should have. He was my life and, for the most part, I was his. Yet, while I entrusted the professionals to care for my son, I let my guard down.

I called the neurologist to tell him that Derek wouldn't be able to make his EEG because he died. The doctor quickly got the MRI report and told me that Derek didn't have a seizure. He sent the report in the mail and when I opened the envelope and read it the tears just streamed down my face. The MRI indicated that he had Periventricular Leukomalacia, which is a thinning of white brain matter and that a lack of oxygen at birth was the cause of his "ABCDEFG" disorder. It was the answer we looked for all of his life.

Three months later on New Year's Eve, the phone rang. "Mrs. Stroh, this is the secretary from the Health Department. Derek's autopsy report is complete. Of course, you know your son died of natural causes; we found no drugs in his system. I'm sorry Mrs. Stroh, your son died from cardiac arrest due to an arrhythmia and the secondary cause was Thyroiditis."

Charlie and I had learned that the so-called "seizure" he had in August was cardiac involved, but the mention of Thyroiditis threw me. After all those years of speaking with doctors about Derek's overeating, obsession with food, the redness in his face and excessive sweating, it took a coroner to diagnose him.

The secretary apologized for calling on New Year's Eve and expressed her condolences. I hung up the phone and began screaming and crying.

It took sometime before I gained any semblance of composure, then took the deep meditative breaths our grief counselor taught us and stared into open space for a while.

***

Before we kissed our son goodbye, Charlie and I had read a eulogy from our seats; each taking a paragraph at a time as we cried through the words,

"He received so much support and love from his teachers and the specialists and, as time went on, his connection with Kids Together was his grounding. He loved being in a group because it was a safe, creative environment and he did a lot of work coming out of his shell. He loved going to the YMCA to be with his friends.

Yes, he loved games and his TV and skiing and all those things boys "like Derek" enjoy, but most of all, I can really say, he loved us. Some say maybe he was too close to us emotionally; he had no qualms about rubbing my back, holding my hand, holding my head, looking in my eyes and planting a kiss. He hugged often and sometimes he'd hug a little too hard.

Life wasn't always easy. We had many struggles and sometimes more obstacles than could be bared, but our pursuit was to make him a happy man.

Within the last few weeks, particularly after our vacation and what we thought was his first seizure, he changed. I think he finally realized how important life is and subconsciously decided to take a big step. He seemed more consistent, willing to enter conversations with us, wanted to help, decided he needed to learn how to skateboard and started lessons. In the meantime, he was convinced that getting healthier and more focused would help him socially so he decided to work with a mentor to establish those goals and we were so proud of him.

We don't know what took him from us and we don't know why. I just know that when he left us he died a warrior.

There are so many people who have played a special role in his life, and you know who you are. We thank all of those who worked, loved, and treasured him as a friend. We love him very much and thank you for being there for him.

We do have a special request though; that is, if you see a kid like Derek, please try to understand and know that they need to be loved just like anyone else and give them your hand."

And that, my friends, is the reason for my story.

About the Author

Pat Stroh entered un-chartered waters when she was encouraged to write a memoir characterizing her son, the trials and tribulations of raising a child with special needs, and the people who were entrusted with his care. To date, her most prolific work has been that of an advocate for her son.

After decades of living in the Catskill Mountains of New York, she and her husband pulled up roots and now reside in New Bern, NC.

ALL THINGS THAT MATTER PRESS

FOR MORE INFORMATION ON TITLES AVAILABLE FROM
ALL THINGS THAT MATTER PRESS, GO TO
http://allthingsthatmatterpress.com
Or, contact us at
allthingsthatmatterpress@gmail.com

**If you enjoyed this book, please post a review on Amazon.com and
your favorite social media sites.
Thank you!**